10

MINUTE GUIDE TO

TEAMS AND TEAMWORK

by John A. Woods

alpha
books

Macmillan Spectrum/Alpha Books

A Division of Macmillan General Reference
A Simon & Schuster Macmillan Company
1633 Broadway, New York, NY 10019-6785

International Standard Book Number: 0-02861739-8
Library of Congress Catalog Card Number: 97-071167

99 98 97   8 7 6 5 4 3 2 1

Interpretation of the printing code: the rightmost double-digit number is the year of the book's first printing; the rightmost single-digit number is the number of the book's printing. For example, a printing code of 97-1 shows that this copy of the book was printed during the first printing of the book in 1997.

Printed in the United States of America.

This is a CWL Publishing Enterprises Book developed for Macmillan Spectrum/Alpha Books.

Publisher: Theresa Murtha

Editor in Chief: Richard J. Staron

Production Editor: Mitzi G. Foster

Cover Designer: Dan Armstrong

Designer: Glenn Larsen

Indexer: Chris Barrick

Production Team: Kim Cofer, Tricia Flodder, Daniela Raderstorf, Rowena Rappaport

CONTENTS

INTRODUCTION

Organizations of all sorts seem to feel that teams are the solution to whatever problem they have, and that's not completely wrong. But the performance improvements that managers seek when they decide to jump on the team bandwagon just don't happen automatically. Teamwork takes work. What kind of work? The answer to that question is what this book is all about.

As you read it, you'll learn about the teamwork attitude and values, which are just as important for team success as any actions managers or team members take. You'll also learn about the different types of teams and roles required for teams to function efficiently.

Leadership in management and in the team is another vital component of success, especially when teams are just getting off the ground. Communication, good interpersonal relations, and effective ways of dealing with conflict are also important if team members are to cooperate in a productive manner. You'll find good ideas on all these subjects in this book as well.

An important reason organizations develop teams is because they are more effective at managing and improving processes. Doing that well requires that team members have some familiarity with process management tools. There are lots of these; however, the purpose of this book is not to provide detailed instruction in how they all work. Instead, you will get an introduction to the most important tools teams use to collect and analyze data and make sound decisions.

It is indeed true that teamwork takes work, but this book will help ease the burden.

CONVENTIONS USED IN THIS BOOK

This book uses the following three types of icons to help you quickly find important information:

Timesaver Tip icons offer ideas that cut corners and avoid confusion.

Plain English icons appear to define new terms.

Panic Button icons identify potential problem areas and how to solve them.

ACKNOWLEDGMENTS

This book came to be at the request of Dick Staron, editor-in-chief at Macmillan General Reference. I want to thank Dick for his support during its development. I thank you for selecting this book to help learn about how to positively affect the motivation of the people you work with and your own at the same time.

DEDICATION

This book is dedicated to my wife Nancy Woods, my partner, friend, and teammate.

THE AUTHOR

John A. Woods is a writer who specializes in the field of business, with special emphasis on issues dealing with quality management and systems thinking. He is the co-author of *QualiTrends: 7 Quality Secrets that Will Change Your Life,* and the *McGraw-Hill Encyclopedia of Quality Terms and Concepts.* He is also co-editor of *The Quality Yearbook* and *The ASTD Training and Performance Yearbook.*

1

WHY TEAMS?

In this lesson, you will learn about work as process, organizations as systems, and why teams make sense for improved performance.

WORK AS PROCESS

If you were to examine how work gets done in any organization, from an airline to a zoo and everything in between, you would see it happens as process.

 Process includes the steps involved in transforming a set of inputs into outputs.

We can analyze *all* work in terms of the steps people go through to change inputs into some output. In organizations, these outputs are always created for customers who will use our outputs to fulfill a need or want they have. For example, a factory takes in raw materials and parts and uses machines and people to create outputs to sell to customers. Figure 1.1 illustrates a process.

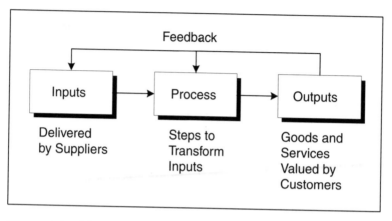

Figure 1.1   **All work can be understood as processes for trans-forming inputs into outputs for customers.**

In addition to steps, the other thing that's important to appreciate about a process is that each step's success partly depends on the successful completion of those that precede it. In other words, step 3 depends on the correct execution of steps 1 and 2. And the employees responsible for steps 1 and 2 need feedback from those responsible for step 3 on whether they are receiving what they need to do their jobs properly. And those executing steps 1 and 2 have to assume the person responsible for step 3 will do it right. Otherwise their work has no purpose.

All the people involved in executing a process depend on one another for its successful completion and to give meaning to their work. A mistake anywhere in the process affects everyone in one way or another.

WHY THINGS GO WRONG IN PROCESSES

Spend some time reflecting on how mistakes happen and why things go wrong at work. If you do this, you'll find that it usually happens because there was a breakdown in a process somewhere. Perhaps people downstream failed to communicate what they expected from the people upstream.

 The terms **upstream** and **downstream** refer to when a process' steps take place relative to one another. An upstream step precedes a downstream step. If someone improperly executes an upstream step, it will negatively affect the downstream steps that follow it.

For example, perhaps someone didn't deliver what you expected when you expected it. Or maybe they delivered something that did not meet specifications. Or maybe a vital machine broke down because it wasn't properly maintained and that affects the entire process.

You might not have thought about your work and the work of your organization in terms of process, but that's the best way to understand it. And if you were to boil down all the reasons things go wrong at work, you would find it's because of a breakdown in cooperation among people executing various steps in a process they are part of.

In other words, when people do not actively cooperate with one another on work that requires cooperation (and almost all work does), there are going to be problems.

WHY DON'T PEOPLE COOPERATE BETTER?

There are various reasons why people don't cooperate well at work. One is that they aren't aware of this idea of work as process. In many organizations, managers and employees simply don't think about the fact that the quality of their individual work depends on the quality of the work of others.

Another reason is that management evaluates people, not in terms of their ability to cooperate and work well with others, but on their individual performance. For example, the salesperson's job is to sell as much as possible even if it creates problems for those in manufacturing because they don't have the capacity to deliver what has been promised. The warehouse is supposed to keep inventory low even if this means a shortage of important parts for maintaining machines. And so on.

The point is that people aren't paid to cooperate. There is no emphasis on communicating and understanding how their work is interdependent. This doesn't change the fact that their work is interdependent. It just means that there will be breakdowns, mistakes, compromised quality, and extra costs because the processes don't work as well as they could.

Remember, people do what they are recognized for. If teamwork is important, you should recognize people (and the whole team for that matter) for being good team players. If people don't get positive feedback for cooperating well, teamwork won't become a positive value for them.

THE ORGANIZATION AS A SYSTEM

We've been examining work in terms of process, but from a larger perspective we are learning to understand the organization as a system. There are many definitions of a system, but for our purposes let's consider it as something we create to produce or deliver something we value. The following are some examples of systems and what they do:

- An airline is a system for delivering fast, efficient transportation.
- A restaurant is a system for creating meals.
- A printing plant is a system for delivering magazines and books, among other things.
- A construction company is a system for building things.

Each of these systems takes in inputs of various sorts, transforms them in ways that customers will value and pay for, and then delivers outputs to these customers. Systems do this work through the processes that were described previously. So think about this:

- There is no organization that is not a system.
- There is no organization in which work does not get done in terms of processes.
- There is no organization in which the work of everyone is not interdependent in some way.

What this means is that if you want to make your system work well, you need, for lack of a better term, *teamwork*. The organization needs to consciously foster a sense of working together to achieve individual, group, and organizational objectives.

Figures 1.2 and 1.3 show the difference between how systems operate when people are aware of the need for cooperation and when they are not. A well-operating system minimizes miscommunication and people working as if they were a bunch of independent contractors.

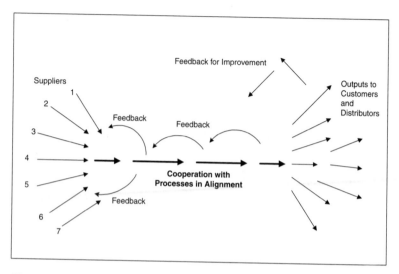

Figure 1.2   A smooth-running system.

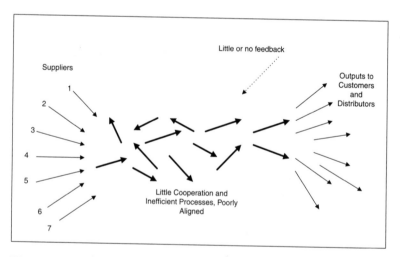

Figure 1.3   A system view of a traditional organization with poorly aligned and inefficient processes.

In a poorly operating system, people are doing their best, but they are often kept in the dark about how their performance affects that of others and the entire organization. This results in people working at cross purposes with one another and the problems mentioned previously.

 Teamwork is both an attitude and a set of actions. The *teamwork attitude* reminds people that everyone's work is interdependent, and the success of the entire organization requires that people cooperate with each other. *Teamwork actions* involve everyone in (1) understanding the whole process and its goals, (2) understanding their individual roles in the process, (3) communicating openly and regularly with one another, and (4) having joint responsibility to execute, as well as continuously improve, the process.

THE IMPORTANCE OF THE TEAMWORK ATTITUDE

The idea of setting up teams in organizations has been a hot management idea for the past several years. Top managers, always on the lookout for solutions to the problem of improving productivity, decide to set up teams. A memo is then issued declaring that this or that group of workers is now a "team."

They hope that this will result in reduced costs and higher-quality work. These managers may even bring in a consulting company to train people in various teamwork skills, such as communication, meeting skills, team decision-making, and so on.

However, there is often one problem in all this. These managers have an attitude problem. They fail to "get" this idea of the organization as a system. They still have a tendency to treat people as if they were those independent contractors mentioned previously. They have not yet adopted the teamwork attitude.

It quickly becomes apparent to workers that calling them a "team" is just another management gimmick that doesn't result in any changes in the way they are managed. The company still doesn't have a good understanding of its processes. And it hasn't put a high premium on the cooperation and communication necessary for teams to operate effectively. The result is mediocre cooperation and not much change from how things were done before.

Unless managers deeply understand and buy into the idea of the organization as a system, calling groups of workers teams simply won't make any difference. There has to be an attitude shift where managers see that taking actions that facilitate cooperation and collaboration among people throughout the organization is the way to improve performance.

So if you are a manager and have heard that teams are the way to go, think deeply about the idea of the organization as a system. Successful teams are based on this idea. Without a good understanding of the organization as a system, teamwork and setting up teams won't really make much sense to you.

You might be moved to declare that workers are now members of teams because you heard that's a good idea, but you won't behave differently in how you manage your employees. And without behavior changes that emphasize teams and teamwork, workers won't change their behavior either.

Workers always take their cues from managers about how they are to behave and what they are to believe. Managers may declare "we are all members of teams" but not change their behavior to bring about better cooperation. Workers will always believe what managers do rather than what they say. Saying one thing and doing another breeds cynicism among workers and undermines the organization's effectiveness.

In this lesson, you learned about work as process, organizations as systems, and why teams make sense to help organizations operate efficiently and deliver higher-quality outputs. In the next lesson, you'll learn about the five teamwork values.

TEAMWORK VALUES

In this lesson, you'll learn about the five teamwork values required to assure that people participate effectively as teammates.

FOUNDATION OF TEAMWORK VALUES

In Lesson 1, we discussed the idea of the organization as a system and work as process. Seeing an organization reinforces that the work of everyone is in some degree interdependent and has the purpose of delivering outputs that customers will value. An important goal of all organizations is to make sure these outputs are high quality, meet the needs and expectations of customers, and have the lowest cost possible.

All this means that if work is interdependent and if you want to keep costs low and quality high, then you need to implement actions that will:

- facilitate people working together (in other words, instill a sense of teamwork in everyone)

- minimize waste and rework (in other words, manage your processes so outputs always meet or exceed specifications with little waste from making mistakes)

These two ideas go together. Teamwork facilitates the efficient management of processes. And the efficient management of processes suggests that you have to get people to really work well with each other.

WHY YOU NEED VALUES THAT SUPPORT TEAMWORK

People behave in ways that are consistent with their values. Values are what people believe to be right, good, true, desirable, correct, moral, and so on. Everyone has a set of values they have learned through experience and education to be correct for them.

 Values are beliefs people hold about what is right, moral, just, and so on. They serve as guideposts for how to behave in different situations.

Sometimes we are not conscious of our values, but think for a moment about why you behave in certain ways and make certain decisions. Ask the question, "What do these behaviors and decisions say about what I value?" Answering this question will help you learn more about why you do what you do.

In an organization where teamwork is not practiced well, you might find managers blaming individuals when outputs don't meet specifications. This would indicate values such as:

- If I do a good job, that's all I have to worry about.

- Problems are the result of somebody messing up.

- Individuals who make mistakes have to suffer the consequences.

Such values would explain the actions of managers who blame individuals when things go wrong. They would help explain why an organization would not practice teamwork. However, they also ignore the idea of the organization as a system and work as process, and therefore they undermine teamwork. In such organizations, we can expect that there will be lots of mistakes made. We can expect a low level of morale. And we can expect a lot of waste and rework.

If you don't have values in place that support teamwork, your teams will not perform well. It's like a sports team where everyone wants the spotlight. Members of such a team don't play well together. They always lose to other teams whose focus is on teammates collaborating with each other to make everyone look good.

The question becomes, if teamwork is required for organizations to do their best, why would you want to have values that are not consistent with helping people collaborate with one another? The answer is, you wouldn't.

But because many managers don't understand the idea of the organization as a system, they behave in ways that compromise the performance of individual employees, themselves, and the organization as a whole. The values we are going to review now will help you avoid such behaviors and help you and everyone perform better.

Teamwork Value 1: We're All in This Together—Company, Customers, and Suppliers

This is the foundation value for teams and teamwork. It emerges naturally from the idea of the organization as a system. If we are all in this together, then our individual success depends on our mutual success and vice versa.

If you really believe the value "we're all in this together," when something goes wrong, your first inclination won't be to find the culprit who messed up. And when the organization is successful, you will take actions to share the rewards of that success and to recognize that everyone played a part.

In other words, this value reinforces the idea of teams and teamwork as the way to get things done. It then suggests that management take actions that establish teams and reinforce the importance of teamwork in all their decisions.

Anytime you try to blame a team member for something that goes wrong rather than looking at how the whole team was working together, you undermine that person's sense of feeling a part of the team. You also send a message to everyone that individual performance is more important than team performance.

TEAMWORK VALUE 2: NO SUBORDINATES OR SUPERIORS ALLOWED

Organizationally, this may sound controversial as it suggests that everyone is equal in rank and authority, but this is not exactly what I mean. Remember we are talking about the teamwork *attitude* here, so this value has to do with how people view and interact with one another.

The existence of people who consider themselves superiors over others means they will treat others as subordinates. What happens? This closes down communication and restricts how these two groups of people relate to each other. On the other hand, the idea that employees are colleagues or teammates also affects how they relate to each other, and this approach fosters open communication and support of one another's efforts.

 One way to demonstrate Teamwork Value 2 is to have the title of associate or teammate or partner for all employees. This helps communicate that the effort of all employees associated in a common enterprise is necessary for everyone to succeed.

DIFFERENT LEVELS OF RESPONSIBILITY, BUT ONE LEVEL OF ATTITUDE

This value does not mean that some people may not have more responsibility than others, nor does it mean that some people may not be assigned to oversee processes on which several people are working. It has everything to do with attitude and approach to this kind of responsibility.

This value suggests to everyone that the work of all members of the team and of the company adds value to the final outputs. It says we are going to focus on the reason we are all here: To better serve our customers and generate the profit we need to stay in business and grow.

When a company's managers eliminate the superior-subordinate attitude and replace it with the idea that we are all teammates, everyone feels more open to express what's on their minds. Everyone will come to appreciate that all employees have something to contribute. They will come to see that it makes sense to create an environment that:

- maximizes rather than restricts an employee's contribution
- facilitates cooperation in executing processes

TEAMWORK VALUE 3: OPEN, HONEST COMMUNICATION IS VITAL

Can you recognize this situation? You're in a conversation and as the other person is talking, you're mainly thinking about what you're going to say next—basically trying to assert your point of view. The other person is probably doing the same thing while you're speaking. Or perhaps you have a colleague who is not doing a good job, but to be polite you feel you just can't say anything. These are examples of dishonest communication that get in the way of teamwork. For teams to prosper, teammates need to be able to speak candidly with one another.

EMPATHY

One aspect of Teamwork Value 3 is empathy. Empathy has to do with proactively seeing the world from the viewpoint of others. These others can be your teammates, suppliers, customers, or members of other departments. Having empathy means to have an appreciation of their problems, abilities, the pressures on them, and their behaviors. It incorporates a reluctance to judge too quickly the ideas and behaviors of others based on your own perspective to the exclusion of theirs. Without empathy, you close yourself off from others in ways that limit your ability to communicate and collaborate with them. With empathy, on the other hand, you do the opposite: you open yourself up to hearing what others have to say. And in so doing, create an environment where they do the same for you.

LISTENING

Along with empathy comes listening. Sometimes it's really hard to listen to others. People try to tell us what's on their minds, and we constantly see incongruencies with our approach to the same subject. We want to correct them or show them how we are right and they are wrong. Behaving in this way is natural. We each have a view of things, and we use that view as a filter to interpret and judge what others have to say and what they do.

Listening, however, has to do with turning down that filter and just hearing what others have to say as representing their perspective. If you can do this, you create a situation where others do the same, as they naturally imitate your behavior.

A simple way to assure that open communication is the norm is simply to always tell the truth. Don't try to distort a situation or withhold information. But be sensitive to the feelings of others. Express yourself in ways that focus on patterns of interaction rather than the behavior of any single person.

As you can probably see, empathy and listening go together. These two characteristics naturally facilitate the open and honest communication that characterizes high performing teams. If you are empathetic, you help create an environment that discourages game playing and deception in communication. And if you listen well, you help create a situation where people will tell you what's on their minds and better listen to what you have to say. All this is why making this one of the teamwork values is important.

TEAMWORK VALUE 4: EVERYONE HAS OPEN ACCESS TO INFORMATION

Part of effective decision making at any level of an organization has to do with the information a person has. Today, information technology makes it possible for all employees to push a few buttons and have access to any information they need to do their jobs.

High-performing companies recognize the importance of sharing information. They understand that limited information means that decisions will be based on speculation rather than facts. Such decisions will be more likely to bring about actions that can result in costly mistakes. Because these companies want to (1) get the most out of their employees, and (2) minimize mistakes, they recognize that making lots of information about operations available just makes sense.

There will always be an element of uncertainty in any decision. People can never predict exactly what's going to happen when they do something. But managers don't have to make this uncertainty worse by withholding information from employees who need it to effectively contribute to organization processes.

Information Facilitates Cooperation

Another reason for sharing information is that it facilitates cooperation. How can people identify with their fellow employees (at all levels of the hierarchy) and cooperate with them if they don't all have access to the same information? The answer is, they can't. And without a common identity among people across the organization, they can't cooperate as well as they might. Because systems depend on cooperation for smooth functioning, this compromises the performance of everyone.

Without open access to and sharing of information among team members, among different teams, and across departments, organizations invite problems. Try exploring why employees might work at cross purposes with one another. One common reason is that they didn't have the information about each other's operations they needed. This is information that may have been available, but they didn't know about it or they didn't have access to it.

DOES EVERYONE NEED TO KNOW EVERYTHING?

This value does not mean that employees need to receive reports every week or month containing all kinds of information they may not need to do their daily jobs. It does mean they have access to any and all information as they need it. And it means they are aware of what's available and are responsible for taking advantage of this information.

The bottom line is that when there are no secrets, employees and teammates don't have to wonder about what's going on in the organization. They can go about doing their jobs in an informed fashion. This makes it much easier for employees and teammates to take into consideration the needs of each other as they do their work. Finally, when all employees, through a sharing of information, understand how their work affects that of others, they naturally collaborate better.

This is the point of Teamwork Value 4. If you want your team and the whole system to operate well, you have to make sure there is shared information that forms the foundation of intelligent decisions, behavior, interaction, and cooperation.

 "I didn't know." That's a common reason for why people make mistakes. Organizations that focus on teamwork and process management know that they can reduce mistakes simply by keeping people informed. Efficiency, effectiveness, and good teamwork are all positively correlated with open access to information.

If you have come to believe that power is associated with hoarding of information, that's not correct. What is associated with information hoarding is mediocrity.

TEAMWORK VALUE 5: FOCUS ON PROCESSES

Lesson 1 emphasized the idea of work as process. Still many managers tend to forget this and focus on the behavior of individuals separate from the system and its processes as the key to success. The purpose of making this a teamwork value is to make sure it doesn't happen.

Here's the difference between a focus on individuals and a focus on processes. Consider some employees who work in a farm implement plant. With a focus on individual work, if you asked employees what they did, you might get answers like this: "I run a drill" or "I run a punch press." In other words, they would talk about this as a generic skill and not the purpose this skill was put to. In a process and teamwork-oriented organization, the answers might be "I help make frames" or "I help make axles." These answers suggest that the employees view their work in terms of the processes by which frames or axles get made.

The fact is that with a focus on individuals and generic skills or a focus on processes, these employees were helping to make frames and axles. However, with the former attitude, managers are not acknowledging this and with the latter they are. If employees somehow feel separate from the processes they are part of, those processes aren't going to work as well as they can. What you want is for all employees to understand:

- that their work is vital

- that others depend on them

- that they are contributing to delivering high-quality outputs for customers

If that sounds like teamwork, that's because it is.

 Work in any organization can always best be defined as collaboration to execute processes. Anytime people forget this, it will cause problems because they will not take into account as well as they should how their work affects others.

So this is why Teamwork Value 5 is important. It reminds people that contributing to processes is at the heart of all organizational work. And this requires cooperation and collaboration. In other words, a focus on processes is the most realistic position you can take. And it, like the other values we have been reviewing, just naturally facilitates the teamwork necessary to have high-performing individuals, teams, and organizations.

PUTTING THEM ALL TOGETHER

All of the values we've reviewed in this lesson are necessary for teamwork to flourish. Proactively adopting these values helps assure that people will have the right attitude about being on a team and working as a teammate. Remember the important point from the beginning of this lesson: People behave in ways that are consistent with their values. If you want teams on the job to be successful, you need values in place that support that.

It's really not so hard to adopt the values listed here. The fact is that they all are enfolded into each other. You can't choose one of them without choosing them all. And if you try, it won't work. All that will happen is disarray and all the problems that occur when people don't collaborate and mutually support one another.

 Mutual respect among teammates is the natural outcome of appreciating that individual success depends, in the final analysis, on team success.

If you want the team to operate effectively, then you have to consciously acknowledge that everyone really is in this together. It doesn't make sense to let superior and subordinate role playing get in the way of working well together. It becomes clear that open communication and ready sharing of information is important. And by a focus on process, you help make sure that everyone knows what they're at work to do— make their contribution to effectively executing that process.

How does this all happen? By people working together as teammates. And what helps assure that that will happen? Having values in place like those covered in this lesson.

In this lesson, you learned about the five teamwork values required to assure that people participate effectively as teammates. In the next lesson, you will learn about some basic characteristics of teams.

SOME TEAM BASICS

3

In this lesson, you will learn about some basic roles and skills needed for people to perform effectively as members of a team.

In general, all teams operate in similar ways. They all depend on people who have a shared goal cooperating with one another to execute the processes necessary to achieve that goal. With that said, experience has taught us that for teams to perform well, they have to be set up properly. This set up includes making sure certain team roles are filled, the team is the right size, and the team has people with the skills needed to achieve its goals.

A **team** is a small group of people who have a distinct identity and work together in a coordinated and mutually supportive way. They are accountable to each other, and they use complementary skills to fulfill a common purpose or goal.

UNDERSTANDING WHAT A TEAM IS

The Plain English definition of a team suggests several things about teams. Let's review those.

TEAM SIZE

The idea of small group means that size affects the ability of team members to work well together. Researchers who have studied teams have found that the best size is 6 to 12 members. This is not absolute, but it suggests that when teams get much larger than this, it becomes more difficult to interact in an efficient manner. And if they're much smaller, this indicates the task before the team is relatively minor.

When thinking about teams, remember the "7 plus or minus 2 rule." Human beings have the capacity to keep straight about 7 plus or minus 2 items at any one time. For team size, this is also true and is a good rule when considering the development of teams for any purpose. As with any rule, however, it is not absolute.

A team with 20 or more members, for example, means that in meetings it can be complicated for everyone to fully participate. If a process requires that many people to execute, and the company has implemented teams, the best thing to do is to break the process up into two parts and have two teams, who work closely together. In that case, the team leaders take on the responsibility of coordinating interaction between the teams.

MUTUAL RESPONSIBILITY

Our definition of a team also suggests that team members have mutual responsibility for executing processes to achieve a goal.

For example, the preparation of this book brought the author, the acquisitions editor, technical reviewer, copy editor, production editor, and marketing personnel all collaborating as a team to deliver the final product to you. Each of us has a role to play, and if we don't do what's expected of us, it affects the performance of the others and can undermine the success of the product, and thus the success of our team, that of the publishing company, and that of the customer who doesn't get the benefits we are seeking to deliver.

MUTUAL ACCOUNTABILITY

Finally, the definition of team suggests mutual accountability, which means understanding that each team member has some responsibility for the team's success. When there are problems, they look not at their individual efforts, but at the interactions and relationships that define their processes for getting things done.

If there's a breakdown, it can almost always be addressed by examining the process and making improvements in the way it operates. For example, if a road crew is repairing pot holes, and there is an equipment problem, the team and its leader do not look for *who* to blame for this. Rather everyone looks at the *what* and *how* of their processes: *What* weakness in current processes led to them not properly maintaining this equipment? And *how* can they can change their processes to minimize this from happening in the future?

Don't ever blame a team member for problems that may occur. No team member ever intentionally makes a mistake. All members base their actions on assumptions they believe to be correct. Problems are less likely to occur when everyone operates from the same assumptions. Some key questions to ask when there are breakdowns are "What assumptions are we each working from?" and "What can we learn from this experience to make sure this problem doesn't happen again?"

TEAM PURPOSE

Teams don't exist because they are nice to have or because some consultant said it's a good idea. Implementing formally recognized teams makes sense because they facilitate the interaction necessary to deliver products and services to internal or external customers. If you don't need a team to do that, then it won't make sense to set them up and invest in all the time and training to get them performing well.

An **internal customer** is another person, group, or team inside the organization who depends on the outputs of another team to do their work. Most teams in an organization serve the needs of internal customers.

An **external customer** is the person or company who actually buys the products or services of an organization. In the final analysis, everyone in the organization plays some role in satisfying external customers, even if they never have direct contact with them.

TEAM LEADERSHIP

A team needs a leader. This is a leader in the best sense of this term and in no way means the team needs a "boss." A team leader does not tell others on the team what to do. This is the person who, through his or her position in the organization, helps set the direction for the team. The leader helps the team get the resources and information it needs to do its work.

A **team leader** is the person responsible for assuring that people will want to work together to achieve a goal or objective. The important idea here is *want to work together*. So a leader does not coerce, but rather facilitates the cooperation necessary for the team to perform well.

The leader is a role model for the other members. By the leader's willingness to cooperate and collaborate with others, he or she sets the tone for how others also cooperate and collaborate. This is the person around whom the other members rally when there is a team problem to solve. Rather than having power, the team leader works hard at empowering others. Finally, the team leader is also the person who helps keep the team focused on its goals.

Often the team leader will be a supervisor. But the leader might also be someone who just naturally emerges from the group. Or it is a person who has a big stake in a project and has been assigned by management to lead the team.

TEAM ROLES

For a team to perform well, there are certain roles that must be filled. As we review these roles, you will see how and why they are important.

A **role** involves an expected set of behaviors and tasks to perform for someone occupying a particular position on a team.

- **Sponsor.** The sponsor is the manager or managers who have set up or empowered the team. Often the sponsor will be a top manager or a highly-placed middle manager. A sponsor is not actually a member of the team, but has the following responsibilities: remove barriers, sanction training, ensure implementation, monitor performance, and provide long-term support, recognition, and rewards.

It's important for the sponsor to be very supportive of the team. Even when things don't go well on a project, the sponsor has to remain committed to the team. In this way, the team will not get discouraged or cynical, will learn from its experience, and become a high performing unit. Without such support, this won't happen.

- **Facilitator.** These are "team experts" who help the team get started and serve as a resource to help the team function as a team. They may not be well informed about the specific work of the team and are really ex-officio members.

  In team meetings, they assist the team leader, performing such tasks as: helping to make sure everyone has a voice, including the "quiet" members, keeping the team on target and moving toward its goals, serving as process experts, and providing stability for the team. This is a role that requires neutrality, empathy, and an understanding of group dynamics and the stages of team development we discussed earlier. In companies that are implementing total quality management, this person might have the title "quality advisor."

- **Team Leader.** Usually a sponsor appoints a team leader or the team itself selects its leader. Sometimes the team just comes together and over time a natural leader emerges. This is usually someone who clearly has the benefit of the entire team in mind and goes out of the way to facilitate cooperation and communication among members.

  Team leaders are responsible for: calling and conducting meetings, preparing for meetings, setting up the agenda and physical space, participating with other members in discussing agenda items and making decisions, serving as official record keepers of all documents that come to or from the team, representing the team to management, and serving as the interface with other teams and departments, such as human resources. Team leaders need to keep the team focused on its goals and help members maximize their contribution. Part of their work includes removing roadblocks that get in the way of team performance.

- **Team Member.** These are the people who are "experts" in the activities in which the team is engaged and who do the work. In addition, team members do the following: share their experience and knowledge with other members, work with other members to standardize and document processes, and work with others to identify ways processes can improve and collaborate to make those improvements.

SOME BASIC TEAMWORK SKILLS

Teams are always organized around some process. For example, a team may be responsible for part of a manufacturing process or for the development of new products. To do their work team members need a variety of skills. There are four categories of skills that are common to all teams:

- **Functional/Technical Skills.** For any team to do its work, its members must have expertise in the skills required to do the work. For example, if a team is constructing a house, you better make sure team members have skills in carpentry, electricity, plumbing, and similar areas.

- **Interpersonal Skills.** The ability to get along with people in general and other members of the team in particular is clearly a vital skill to facilitate teamwork. Even one member of a team who doesn't get along well with others can disrupt and distract the energies of a whole team. Training in teamwork often includes information and exercises aimed at helping improve their interpersonal skills.

- **Problem-Solving Skills.** Processes never operate without problems and without opportunities to make improvements. There are several tools and techniques team members can use to better understand processes, identify the causes of problems, and make improvements. This is another area in the curriculum of teamwork training.

- **Decision-Making Skills.** Team members need to attain consensus around a course of action. This means they have to know how to work together to identify options and come to shared agreement on which options make the most sense. There are several techniques for doing this, and we will cover the most important of these later in this book.

In this lesson, you learned about some basic roles and skills needed for people to perform effectively as members of a team. In the next lesson, you will learn about different types of teams in organizations.

DIFFERENT TYPES OF TEAMS

In this lesson, you will learn about the different types of teams often found in organizations and what they do.

You might think a team is a team. However, there are different types of teams. Some of them are relatively permanent, and others are temporary. Some have members from different departments, and some consist of employees from the same department or work area.

WHAT DISTINGUISHES DIFFERENT TYPES OF TEAMS?

There are two general characteristics that distinguish different types of teams:

- The organizational processes they are called on to execute

- How they are managed

Let's review both of these as a foundation for what follows in this lesson.

ORGANIZATIONAL PROCESS DIFFERENCES

Some teams have the responsibility for a particular on-going set of operations and processes. These teams are permanent, with a membership made up of people from the same department. Such a team might be responsible for a part of a manufacturing process, or for the mailroom of an office, or shipping and warehousing. In addition to being charged with executing and monitoring its processes to make sure they run smoothly, these teams are usually accountable for continuously improving these processes.

Other teams are responsible for special projects. Usually these projects are of a temporary nature. They often involve employees from several different departments whose talents are needed to successfully complete the project. Such teams are responsible for designing and executing the processes necessary to successfully complete the project. When it is completed, the team disbands. These are often called cross-functional teams. An example of a cross-functional team might be a group of people who work together to develop a new product or design a new process that will affect many different departments.

A **cross-functional team** is a team with members from different functional areas in an organization who come together to work on a common project or task.

MANAGEMENT DIFFERENCES

In addition to the process that a team is involved with, another major difference between team types is their management. Teams may either have a manager who is responsible for and has authority over the team's actions, or a team may be self-managed. In a self-managed team (also called a self-directed team), there is no manager. Instead, all team members are jointly responsible for the execution of a process. This can include scheduling, purchasing, repairing, interacting with suppliers, and every other activity involved in delivering a product or service to customers.

A **self-managed team** is a group of employees who have the responsibility for an entire process that delivers a product or service to a group of customers.

Self-managed teams are usually found only in organizations that have made a major commitment to the importance of teamwork and have mature teams in place that have the experience and understanding to take responsibility for their processes. In addition, self-managed teams have usually received cross-training in all the different skills required for the entire team to do its work. In this way, members can fill in or help one another to take care of bottlenecks or other problems in the processes for which they are responsible.

Cross-training means providing all members of a team with training in all the different skills for which the team is responsible. This might mean that on a manufacturing process team all team members know how to operate all machines, plus know how to use computers, develop reports, and any other skills involved in that process.

ORGANIZATIONAL PROCESSES AND TEAM TYPES

All the types of teams we are going to review here are associated with specific organizational processes. For each of these processes, it is often the case that setting up a team is the best way to assure that the process will be efficiently and effectively executed.

You'll often hear the words **efficient** and **effective** used when talking about organizational processes. They are both important. If a team is *efficient*, this means it is getting the most outputs for the amount of inputs it's using. In other words, there is minimal waste of time and materials. If a team is *effective*, this means that its outputs are meeting the needs and expectations of customers. Finding ways to improve efficiency and effectiveness is a never-ending task for teams.

Now let's review the different types of teams you might find in companies. (The information in this section is adapted from the work of Peter Scholtes, as described in the article "Teams in the Age of Systems," *Quality Progress*, December 1995, pp. 51–59.)

If individuals are to work well as team members they must receive training in teamwork skills, such as team decision making, holding meetings, communication skills, and the use of tools that allow them to effectively plan, monitor, and improve the processes they are responsible for. Without these skills the team will not function well.

FUNCTIONAL TEAM

A functional team is a permanent team consisting of employees who work together in a single department or functional area to generate some output. Here are some things to know about natural work group teams:

- **Purpose:** This type of team is responsible for establishing, maintaining, and improving certain functional processes involved in delivering a specific output.

- **When To Use This Team:** These teams should be used when a functional process is better done by a team than by individuals. For example, a functional team may not be necessary for the smooth functioning of a customer service group where each person answers the phone. However, a marketing department with its interrelated activities of advertising, promotion, publicity, and sales support could be better performed by a functional team that needs to work closely together to coordinate their actions.

- **Advantages:** Whenever a process or set of interrelated processes requires the cooperation of several people to execute properly, a functional team can help assure this process works better.

- **What To Watch Out For:** Functional teams have to be careful not to become self-absorbed and forget they are part of a larger system that includes lots of other teams they also have to work with.

EXECUTIVE MANAGEMENT TEAM

This is a team of the top managers of the organization who are peers and the CEO. Another way of describing this is that it is the CEO and the people who directly report to him or her.

This is a permanent team. Here are some things to know about an executive management team:

- **Purpose:** To provide coordinated leadership to the organization. When top managers consider themselves to be part of a team rather than running fiefdoms, there will more and better cooperation among departments and divisions to fulfill the organization's mission and objectives.

- **When To Use This Team:** This should be standard operating procedure in all organizations that have executive managers. They should meet regularly and support one another's efforts.

- **Advantages:** Having this type of team builds common purpose in the organization and consensus for strategy and actions. This type of cooperation among top managers also provides a model for behavior at all lower levels in the organization.

- **What To Watch Out For:** This type of team might have a tendency to believe it has the answers and not pay attention to others. It may also grab onto management fads that can divert attention from customers, continuous improvement, and discovering new market opportunities.

A potential problem of any team of managers is that they will want to protect their turf. In this case, the team will be less an exercise in cooperation and teamwork than in making sure individual interests are protected. This is likely to happen if managers do not fully appreciate that organizations are systems, and if teamwork values are not firmly entrenched in the organization.

MIDDLE MANAGEMENT TEAM

This is like an executive management team, except here the membership is made up of the managers of various groups that make up a department or division and the executive who heads it up. It is a permanent team. Here are some things to know about a middle management team:

- **Purpose:** This type of team helps assure constancy and consistency among the actions of the groups who make up a department or division and cooperation with other departments and divisions. It also allows for the quick deployment and collection of information.

- **When To Use This Team:** This should be standard operating procedure in all organizations. The members should meet regularly and support one another.

- **Advantages:** These teams build consensus for common and coordinated action. They also help create a support for each other. And they serve as a role model for how teams at lower levels should function.

- **What To Watch Out For:** Unless teamwork is firmly entrenched, turf battles can break out among managers. They may also forget they are part of a larger system, focusing on only their own performance and not how it contributes to other departments and divisions. There may also be a tendency to avoid conflicts and risks in an attempt to maintain harmony.

PROCESS IMPROVEMENT OR REENGINEERING TEAM

This is a temporary team charged with either analyzing and improving a current process or set of interrelated processes or charged with developing a whole new process to replace the current one. It may include all members from one functional area or it may be a cross-functional team. Here are some things to know about a process improvement team:

 Process improvement teams are often cross-functional in nature because they are called on to help improve how the organization may deliver a particular output and this can affect the functions of several different departments.

- **Purpose:** Process improvement teams do just what their name implies: they look at the processes by which a product or service is delivered, look for redundancies and waste in the process, suggest a new process design, and then work with teams in the affected areas to implement the new design. A process improvement team mainly focuses on incremental improvements to the current process.

- **When To Use This Team:** Whenever a process clearly needs improvement, it's a good idea to create a team of involved employees to undertake the improvement.

- **Advantages:** Involved employees are the most qualified to make process improvements. These employees, being closest to the situation, will build commitment to the revised process.

- **What To Watch Out For:** Process improvement requires skilled use of analysis and improvement tools. Team members need a sound grounding in systems analysis and improvement methodologies. Otherwise, any changes may only introduce new problems into the system.

New Product Design Team

This is usually a temporary, cross-functional team with the responsibility of designing a new product or service. Here are some things to know about a new product development team:

- **Purpose:** Using this type of team allows an organization to bring together all the different people who will be involved in the design, development, manufacture, and delivery of a new product. Working in a team like this allows all departments to have a say, not only in what the product will be like but how it will be manufactured and delivered. The goal is to minimize mistakes that might come from not anticipating problems throughout the chain of events that conclude with a product or service delivered to a happy customer.

- **When To Use This Team:** This type of team is always appropriate for designing innovative new products or services.

- **Advantages:** It gets representatives from all departments involved in ways that can prevent problems and take advantage of what all have to contribute. It also builds commitment among all departments because of its early involvement.

- **What To Look Out For:** It is possible for this type of team to look inward at its ideas without paying enough attention to customers. The team may also become too innovative, adding features that customers won't consider valuable enough as benefits to pay for.

One way to be sure a new product design team does not forget customers is to invite one or more customers to be on the team, at least as ex-officio members. In this way, the team is not likely to forget the customer's needs.

PROJECT TEAM

A project team is a temporary team, either functional or cross-functional, that is set up to design policies or procedures or take on some special project for a customer.

In a manner of speaking, all temporary teams are project teams. This classification just takes in all those areas not covered by the different categories covered already. In some companies, project teams are the norm and employees and managers go from team to team as each project is completed. In this case, being a member of a project team is not something done in addition to one's regular job, but a person's full time job until the project is completed.

- **Purpose:** A project team brings together all the specialties needed to actually plan and execute some special project. For example, when a customer has a special need, a project team will be formed to address this need, including designing, planning, and managing whatever needs to be done to fulfill this need.

- **When To Use This Team:** Anytime a special situation or request from a customer arises or when there is a special internal problem that needs to be addressed, a project team is called for.

- **Advantages:** It brings together people with the expertise needed to address the need or problem in an efficient and effective manner.

- **What To Watch Out For:** Anytime you have a team, it's important that they be trained in teamwork skills and understand how to work together. Otherwise, there will be lack of coordination and conflict as members fail to come together as a team.

In this lesson, you learned about different types of teams—permanent and temporary, functional and cross-functional—and what type of tasks each takes on. In the next lesson, you will learn about the stages a team goes through in evolving into a high performing unit.

5

THE STAGES OF TEAM DEVELOPMENT

In this lesson, you will learn the stages a team goes through as it evolves into a high-performing unit.

High performing teams don't just spring up ready to go. It takes time, energy, experience, and learning for a group of people who come together as a team to learn how to operate as well functioning unit.

Another word for team development is *team building*, and the goal of this is to have a team that can achieve its objectives, that has come together as a team, and that can effectively give each member a chance to contribute in a personally meaningful way.

It's useful for anyone who is trying to start a team or who is going to be a member of one to understand these team development stages. In this way, team members won't have their expectations shattered when things don't go so smoothly at the beginning.

At each stage we can expect different behaviors. Some have to do with getting used to each other. Some have to do with creating modes of working together. And some have to do with getting on with the tasks and objectives for which the team was formed in the first place. In the jargon of teams, the four stages of team development are *forming, storming, norming,* and *performing.*

In general, we can think of the stages of team development in terms of a person's lifespan: toddlerhood to childhood to young adulthood to maturity. Things happen at each stage, but it is only at the maturity stage where performance takes off. Of course, teams move through these stages in a few months, but they will go through them just the same.

STAGE 1: FORMING

Just as the name implies, this is the beginning stage of a team. It's the stage where members start to feel one another out and get to know each other as team members, not just fellow employees. One expert in organization culture calls this the *dependency* stage. The members depend on one another and the leader to provide direction because they aren't sure of themselves.

Members seek to figure out what's expected of them and how they are going to work together effectively. They are asking questions about what their task is and how in the world they are going to organize themselves to achieve this goal.

The forming stage is important because it is the foundation for the team to evolve into a high-performing unit. If the team can articulate a clear sense of purpose for itself, this makes the rest of the stages go more smoothly.

 During the forming stage, the team should create a mission statement for itself. This articulates the team's purpose, who its customers are, and what it will deliver to them. This serves as a foundation on which to move ahead.

STAGE 2: STORMING

In this stage, the members begin to understand their task. They may realize that it is more difficult than they imagined. They still don't have their roles figured out. At this point, it's normal for members to become a little defensive because they are not making progress as quickly they would like. They're not sure how it's all going to work out, and they might become anxious and impatient.

Think of storming like the second stage in learning a new sport, such as golf. Once you've been introduced to the game (the forming stage), you want to play a round. Because you don't have a lot of experience, you start flailing at the ball, sometimes hitting it squarely and straight and sometimes not. To learn the game, this is a necessary step that eventually will lead to competence.

When this uncertainty about the team creeps in, members typically fall back on their personal and professional experiences and seek to push their own views onto the whole group rather than hearing what others have to say. There may be open conflict and competition among team members as different members try to assert their individual viewpoints. The team makes little progress toward achieving its objectives, but members begin to know more about one another. Sometimes this stage is characterized as one of *counterdependency*, suggesting the idea that members resist depending on one another and working together.

The storming stage is difficult, but normal. It's important not to get discouraged and recognize that team members can get through it. It's a disordered stage, but this disorder helps motivate people to seriously organize themselves so they can get beyond this and get down to business.

This storming stage is similar to any situation where we find that we are stuck there and aren't sure where we stand or how to proceed. In such situations, we fall back on our experience, relying on what we know (even if that is only partially relevant) until we get better handle on things. Once we better understand the situation, we can deal with it more effectively.

The storming stage can be lengthy, but members have to stick with it. They will slowly but surely begin to learn how to adapt to each other. They will begin to get a sense of one another's skills and personality and how each person might contribute to achieving the team's goals.

Team members and the team leader can help each other get through this by openly discussing their confusion and uncertainty and how to deal with these in a productive manner.

The storming stage can be short or perhaps even skipped if the team has done a good job at the forming stage of articulating its mission and purpose.

Stage 3: Norming

In this stage, team members begin to reconcile differences among themselves and finally get used to working together. They accept each other, their roles, norms, and expectations. As this happens, the team members' initial resistance to working together fades away and competitive relationships become more cooperative. Team members begin to help each other. Because members can now concentrate on the team's objective, they begin to make measurable progress toward doing this.

In terms of the golf analogy, at this stage, the player has had some lessons, understands how to play, but hasn't had enough practice to score well. With enough practice, however, will come competence.

A **norm** is an accepted way of behaving or standard for behavior that everyone in a group agrees is appropriate for members to get along well and achieve their objectives.

In the norming stage, members begin to appreciate that others have a contribution to make and that they can learn from each other. They start looking at their process for interacting and may set up ground rules for guiding these interactions.

This stage is characterized by the idea of *cohesion*. Members begin to identify with the team and feel a bond with other team members. They want to get things done working together, but are still figuring out how to make that happen.

 The norming stage might not arrive if the team does not have a clear sense of purpose for itself. It can remain in a kind of storming mode if it doesn't have answers to questions like "What are we really expected to do as a team?" and "How are we going to organize and coordinate our efforts to meet our goals?" A clear sense of mission facilitates norming.

STAGE 4: PERFORMING

At this stage, the team members have reconciled most of their differences, and they have become comfortable with each other. They have discovered and they accept each other's strengths and weaknesses.

They communicate openly with one another and have developed methods and techniques for effectively interacting with one another. They know how to constructively disagree with one another and how to resolve these disagreements in ways that lead to productive actions.

You can tell a team has reached this stage because it starts to get a lot of work done, quickly and efficiently. There is now real synergy at work. They all know how they can contribute most effectively and can count on one another.

Another way to characterize this stage is as *interdependency*. They operate like a well-tuned engine, with all the parts working correctly. Members know their role is to contribute to helping the team perform well as a team, and they know how to go about doing this. There is strong feeling of commitment to one another and to their objectives.

Synergy means that team members are cooperating in a way that allows them to accomplish more, sometimes far more, than they could working as individuals without that cooperation.

There is no finger pointing when something goes wrong. If one member has a problem, they consider it the team's problem and work together as a team to solve it. Likewise, when they succeed, the members give credit to the whole team rather than their individual efforts.

Just because a team has reached the performing stage doesn't mean that things won't go wrong, both in terms of its tasks and in members working with one another. However, the team now has mastered the tools and skills members need to deal with both technical and team problems.

At this fourth stage, we have a team performing at a high level. But in making this observation, it's still important to note that they had to go through the stages described here. They had to crawl before they could walk, and they had to walk before they could run. At the performing stage, we can say the team is running well.

Finally, don't forget that high-performing teams are most likely to happen in organizations that have a set of values in place that supports teamwork. Without such values and the supportive culture that goes with them, people will mainly be going through the motions. It's unlikely that the team will ever reach the performing stage.

A team that has reached the performing stage might tend to become complacent and see their performance level off or even decline. The only way to make sure that doesn't happen is to be aware of the possibility and make teamwork and continuous performance improvement a priority.

In this lesson, you learned the stages a team goes through as it evolves into a high performing unit. In the next lesson, you will learn about an effective procedure for planning and holding team meetings.

EFFECTIVE TEAM MEETINGS

In this lesson, you will learn a procedure for planning and holding effective team meetings.

TEAMWORK AND MEETINGS

An important part of teamwork is meeting regularly to review progress, deal with problems, decide on next steps, and make other decisions relevant to the team's work. For meetings to fulfill their purpose, you need a good meeting process.

Many times people complain that meetings are a waste of time. They are unstructured, wander off topic, and last too long. Attendance ends up not making much difference in what people do on a day-to-day basis or in how they work together. This does not have to be the case. You'll find that high performing teams almost always have an agreed-upon process for making meetings productive.

MEETING TYPES

In organizations, there are two types of meetings:

- **Type 1: Ongoing Team Meetings.** Type 1 is a participative meeting with all team members involved in discussing, planning, and deciding on a variety of issues. A participative meeting might have the goals of exchanging information on what people are doing, solving a problem that has come up, and planning next steps on a project.

- **Type 2: Meetings to Inform People.** Type 2 is a nonparticipative meeting, which means that the leader or someone else is giving out information needed by the team members. Type 2 meetings often have to do with human resources policies, financial results, and delivering other information that helps people know what's going on in the organization. They may include questions and answers after the announcement.

A **participative meeting** is one in which all members participate by sharing, discussing, and working with other members to solve problems and reach consensus on future actions. A **nonparticipative meeting** is one in which attendees receive announcements and general information related to their jobs or employment in an organization. There is little discussion in such a meeting.

What we're concerned with in this lesson is the participative meeting. This is the type most often held by teams. What follows is a process for planning and conducting effective team meetings.

The meeting process described here is appropriate for any participative-type meeting you might have to organize, whether it's for a team or one-time gathering of a group in any organization.

THE AGENDA

It's very important that a meeting agenda be prepared and handed out to all participants ahead of time. Try to make sure everyone has the agenda a day or two before the meeting, or at least in the morning if the meeting is to be held in the afternoon. Sometimes this isn't possible, but you should make it a goal.

A complete agenda should include the following elements:

- The *meeting date*; the *meeting time* (start and end times), the *meeting place*, and a *list of participants*, and *items to bring* (if appropriate).

- The *topics to be covered* with the *amount of time* planned for each item.

- *Who is responsible* for that part of the meeting. Often different topics will be the responsibility of different people.

- *How each topic will be covered*. Different topics require different procedures, for example, discussion, brainstorming, round robin, and reporting.

 A **round robin** in a meeting is where the meeting facilitator goes around the table and asks each member to comment on a particular issue. In round robins it's important that each person's comments be kept brief and relevant to the topic at hand.

- *Expected outcome*. For some topics, you might expect something specific to be concluded, such as a plan or a decision. If that's the case, include that as part of the agenda.

While it takes discipline and planning to include all of these items on an agenda, having it planned out like this makes the meeting go more smoothly. For example, you might include who is responsible for each topic or how the topic will be covered, and expected outcomes.

 tip Members may come to know each other and meeting procedures well enough to wait for the beginning of the meeting to decide how to take up each topic. The important thing is that the team have a procedure for taking up each topic.

Overall, the agenda is the meeting plan. A carefully thought-out plan helps assure the meeting will proceed smoothly, and people will be glad to come and participate because they know it will help them work together with their teammates to achieve their mutual objectives.

PARTICIPANT ROLES

There are various roles to fill to make the meeting run smoothly. These include:

- **Meeting owner.** This is often the team leader, but it doesn't have to be. It could be another member who is responsible for certain work and needs to call a meeting with other members who are also involved in this work. The meeting owner is responsible for developing the agenda and setting up the room.

- **Meeting facilitator.** Sometimes the meeting owner may want someone else to run the meeting because the owner wants to participate in the discussion. In this case, there is also a meeting facilitator.

This is someone who can remain relatively neutral on the issues being covered and who is skilled at conducting meetings. This person keeps the team moving through the agenda without getting distracted.

- **Scribe.** This is a person who volunteers at the meeting to record ideas on flip charts that everyone can see. This person should have legible handwriting. The scribe should number ideas as they are written down. Once a sheet is filled, tape it on the wall where it will be visible to everyone. This role can shift from meeting to meeting.

- **Timekeeper.** This is another volunteer who keeps track of how much time is being spent on a topic and helps the team keep to its schedule as noted on the agenda. The timekeeper should warn the team when there are five minutes left, and when time is up on a particular topic. This role shifts from meeting to meeting.

 The timekeeper is an important role. If the team does not abide to the time allotted for a topic, it means their meeting process is not under control. This wastes time and contributes to the overall dislike people have for meetings.

- **Note taker.** This is the person who takes notes, formats them into final minutes, and distributes them to everyone after the meeting. The notes capture what the team members discussed, what decisions they made, and who will do what and by when, and any other information that will serve as a record of the meeting. A different person should do the note taking at each meeting.

 The team leader should maintain a file for all meeting agendas and notes from meetings. In this way, the team can maintain a history of its discussions, agreements, and decisions.

CONDUCTING THE MEETING

The leader or facilitator should stick to the agenda and start the meeting on time. After selecting members to perform the roles of scribe, timekeeper, and note taker, the meeting begins.

Meetings should begin with something called a *check-in*. It's usually a good idea to go around the table and have participants say what they have been working on or personal activities they are spending time on as a way to get the meeting going. It gives everyone a chance to speak, lets participants share with each other what they have been doing, creates and reinforces fellowship among members, and gets people's minds off the activities they have been doing and onto the issues at hand.

The next item is a review of the agenda. This allows for the team to add any items to the agenda that might be appropriate, adjust time devoted to various topics if needed, and get agreement on what the meeting will cover. After that, the meeting proceeds according to the agenda. One important part of meetings is coming to agreement on decisions that affect the team. There are a number of techniques for helping participants do this. We'll review those in Lesson 7.

As meetings proceed, there are any number of obstacles to their productivity. When these obstacles, or meeting killers, make their appearance, it's appropriate for the leader or any participant to say, "It looks like we're stuck in some particular way." Then the team can decide how to resolve the issue and get on with the agenda.

The last item on the agenda is an evaluation of the meeting. A meeting is a process like any other, and it can be improved. Thus, it's a good idea to have everyone say how they thought the meeting went and make any suggestions for improving the process. If there is general enthusiasm about any suggestions, the note taker should make sure that this is in the notes. Then the team leader or other meeting owner should make sure the team implements that improvement in their next meeting. For example, someone may suggest what information should be available when they cover a particular item. Next meeting, make sure that information is there.

In this lesson, you learned a proven procedure for planning and holding effective team meetings. In the next lesson, you will learn about two techniques teams can use to make decisions.

7

TEAM DECISION-MAKING

In this lesson, you will learn two techniques teams can use to come to consensus decisions.

Team decision-making is different from individual decision-making. If a team is to perform as a team, there has to be shared understanding and commitment to objectives and to the methods for achieving those objectives. Otherwise, it is simply a group of employees doing what they're told by a manager.

DECISIONS AND ACTION

What is a decision? A good answer to this question is this: The decisions we make reflect our best understanding of ourselves in relation to the situations in which we find ourselves at the time we make the decision. In other words, our decision really says, "This is how I understand the situation and what I'm going to do in light of that understanding." The choices we make are always consistent with our best understanding of ourselves in relation to the circumstances at the time. The better our understanding, the better our decisions and the subsequent actions.

Sound decisions depend on two things: (1) the amount of good information people have, and (2) the way they interpret that information. The best interpretations always take into account how a decision will promote the effective operation of processes and help to better satisfy customers.

DECISIONS IN TEAMS

Decision-making, then, is the process we go through to come to that understanding. In terms of teams, decision-making involves selecting a course of action to address problems and opportunities they face in doing their work. For the team to operate as a real team, it's very important that members all feel ownership of and commitment to that decision and the actions they must take to implement it.

WHAT DECISIONS DO TEAMS MAKE?

Teams have to make decisions and come to shared understanding about many different issues as they do their work. Here are some examples of the types of decisions that confront teams:

- Team members have to look at the task they are assigned and decide on their plans for how to tackle it. This will usually involve the sequence of steps they might take and a timeline for getting things done.

- As teams proceed with their work, they are going to confront unanticipated problems they will have to address and decide how to handle it.

- As team members go about their work, it's often the case that they come across opportunities, either to serve new customers or make improvements on current techniques, that will require the entire team to discuss and decide on.

- Teams may be required to develop a budget for people, material, equipment, expenses, and so on. They have to decide together on what they need, how much it should cost, and how to responsibly manage their budget.

HOW TEAMS MAKE DECISIONS

Traditionally, people in a group bargain, compromise, and vote, resulting in decisions that no member may fully understand, believe in, or commit to. But without the understanding and commitment of all team members, the decisions don't get implemented or are implemented poorly.

There are tools available that can help team members explore ideas in a way that gets them all involved and working together to make decisions. In using these, they will be acting as a well-coordinated team rather than as individuals who have to work together but with each having his or her own agenda.

The goal in team decision-making is to reach consensus. Consensus means finding solutions to problems and courses of action that all members will find acceptable and support. In team decision-making, reaching consensus will usually result in the best decision for team members and for the organization. This is because members better understand the decisions because everyone participated in making them and because they reflect the concerns and ideas of all team members.

Consensus means reaching decisions that all members of a team accept and support.

In other words, it's much better to have team consensus decisions than decisions made by majority votes or made by the team leader or supervisor alone. Figure 7.1 illustrates the overall quality of team decisions (in terms of participation, commitment, and maximizing the talents of the entire team) as we move from a team leader making the decision to majority rule to consensus.

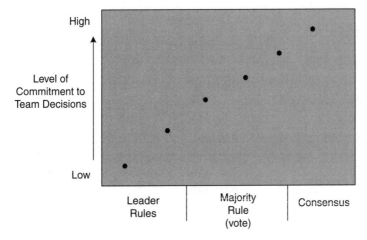

Figure 7.1   The relative commitment of team members based on different decision-making processes. (Adapted from *American Samurai* by William Lareau New York: Warner Books, 1991, p. 289.)

We are going to look at two specific techniques that teams can use to reach consensus decisions.

Consensus decisions are the best, but it's also important that the team not get so bogged down in coming to a consensus that it hinders progress. Another problem is a tendency to look inward at what the team likes and can agree on. The primary focus on all decisions must ultimately be process improvement and customer satisfaction.

BRAINSTORMING WITH MULTIVOTING

Brainstorming is a technique for generating many different ideas for dealing with a situation in a short amount of time. A successful brainstorming session should be freewheeling with no constraints on what members suggest and with no member allowed to criticize the suggestions of other members. Here are some basic guidelines for brainstorming:

 Brainstorming is a technique groups can use to get a lot of ideas out of people quickly.

- Spend about 5 to 10 minutes collecting ideas.

- The scribe records all ideas in each speaker's own words on a flip chart, giving each idea a number.

- No criticisms or judgments about ideas are allowed.

- Members can either take turns giving ideas or call ideas out as they think of them.

- Go for volume of ideas and forget feasibility.

- Build on ideas from each other.

- No discussion of ideas during their generation.

This kind of session often will spark ideas in all members that they probably would not have working alone. Not only does brainstorming work to generate a lot of ideas, it also encourages creativity as members piggyback on each other.

Once the team has collected several ideas, the next step is to pare down the list to a few that seem most useful and that everyone can agree on. Then the members' task is to select one or two that best capture the team's understanding of what action would be most fruitful.

A useful method for doing this is multivoting, a process for the team to select the most important or popular items with limited discussion and difficulty. Here is how it works:

 Multivoting is a technique by which group members vote for several ideas that appeal to them and that allows the team to systematically narrow the possibilities down to those that have the broadest appeal to the entire group.

1. Number all items listed on the flip charts. If two or more ideas are similar, combine them, but only if all members agree.

2. Each team member writes down on a slip of paper the numbers of the items they prefer from the entire list. For example, if there are 50 ideas, each member might write the numbers of 15 to 20 of these. Members should agree ahead of time on the amount of items each member will select. Normally the number would be about one-third as many as are on the entire list.

3. Go down the list and record the number of votes for each item on the list. On a team of eight members, some items may have eight votes, some may have none, or anywhere in between. After tallying the list, eliminate those with the fewest votes. For example, in a team of eight members, eliminate those with three or fewer votes.

4. Go through the procedure again, but this time, each member only selects, say, seven to 10 items until the team has narrowed the list to a small number of items.

5. The team then discusses the selected ideas with the goal of coming to a consensus on their choice and course of action. This may include some combination of the final items.

Coming to consensus after the list has been narrowed by using multivoting usually just evolves out of the discussion as it becomes clear what idea or ideas make the most sense given the team's goals or problem they are dealing with.

This procedure for generating ideas and voting on them is not meant to be rigid. Sometimes members will not be able to come to a consensus decision in one meeting or even two meetings because they need to collect more information. However, they can still use this procedure to come up with a final set of ideas from which they can make their final consensus choice.

NOMINAL GROUP TECHNIQUE

Nominal group technique (NGT) is a structured process to give everyone in a group an equal voice in helping a group decide on a course of action. It is especially useful in situations where some members might seem to dominate in the group or when team members are new to each other.

An advantage of NGT is that it allows a large number of issues to be pared down quickly. A potential disadvantage is that it discourages a lot of discussion. Here are the steps for NGT:

1. Define the problem or opportunity so that everyone agrees on this and understands it. Write this on a flip chart in the front of the room.

2. Generate ideas. Each person individually and silently writes down all his or her ideas on a sheet of paper that address the issue. The amount of time for this should be about five to seven minutes. Team members should write these ideas as short phrases.

3. Record ideas on a flip chart. The leader or facilitator goes around the room taking one idea from each person, continuing around the table several times until all ideas are recorded. Number each item listed.

4. Discuss and clarify ideas. The leader or facilitator goes through each idea, asking if anyone has questions or needs clarification. If possible, combine ideas that are similar.

5. Discuss and agree on criteria for voting on certain items. For example, the idea must be easy to implement, acceptable to management, have a low cost, have a high likelihood of success, and similar criteria.

6. Rank vote the items. Depending on the number of ideas, the members are directed to select a smaller number of these and rank their preference for their selections. For example, if there are 25 ideas, each member selects five. If there are 50 items, each

person selects eight to 10. Here is how voting process works:

- On a set of 3 × 5 cards, each member writes down one selected idea on the middle of a card and the number of the idea chosen in the upper-left corner of the card.

- After selecting the agreed-upon number of ideas, each member then ranks these from most preferred to least preferred. If there are eight items selected, the one *most* preferred is ranked as 8 and so on to the least preferred, which is ranked as 1. Figure 7.2 shows what a card should look like.

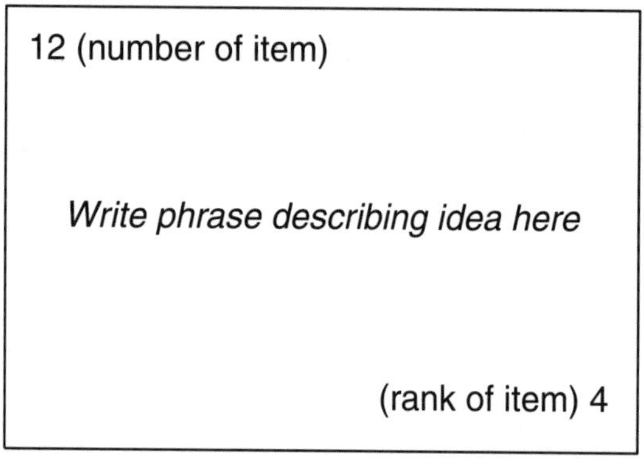

12 (number of item)

Write phrase describing idea here

(rank of item) 4

Figure 7.2   A filled out card for use in the nominal group technique.

7. Collect the cards and tally the vote. The leader goes through and places the numbers showing the rankings for each idea. The final tally might look like this if there were 24 ideas:

1. 4-6-1	9. 6-1	17.
2. 3-8	10. 5-3-8-1	18. 7-2-3
3.	11.	19. 1-3
4.	12. 7-2-4	20.
5. 4-8-7-3-2	13.	21. 2-5
6.	14. 2-5-1	22.
7.	15.	23. 6-4-2
8.	16. 4-7-8-3	24.

8. Add the rankings for each item together, and the one with the highest total is the group's choice. In the preceding list, idea 5 has the highest total with 24. If the vote is close, select the two or three highest vote getters and through discussion come to a consensus about the idea that best meets the group's criteria for acceptance.

While the nominal group technique is a little bit involved, it is a fair and impartial way to arrive at consensus on a problem or opportunity with a minimum of disagreement among members.

 Sometimes a team is more concerned with consensus than making the right decision. Remember to always look at any decision in terms of improving process operation *and* customer satisfaction.

In this lesson, you learned two techniques teams can use to come to consensus decisions. In the next lesson, you will learn about team leadership responsibilities.

TEAM LEADERSHIP

In this lesson, you will learn the special tasks and roles of a team leader that contribute to the success of a team.

The most important characteristic of any team is how team members interact and collaborate together to achieve their goals. Essential to making sure that goes well is an excellent team leader. We can think of the team leader as a kind of first among equals. In the tradition of great leadership, the team leader identifies his or her success with the ability to help the team succeed.

This does not mean that team success lies strictly on the shoulders of the leader. In fact, it is just the opposite—team success depends absolutely on the team as a whole. However, the leader acts as a inspirer, facilitator, and obstacle remover as the team does its work. What follows are some of the ways leaders do this.

LEADER AS ROLE MODEL

The team leader is a role model for all the other members. This is the person who has been charged by management to be the official or nominal head of the team. As such, other team members will naturally look to the leader for cues as to the appropriate way to behave as a team member.

Understanding this, the team leader will go out of his or her way to cooperate and empower other members and share responsibility for executing team tasks. A common reason teams fail to come together and start performing is that the person chosen to lead the team continues to make decisions and direct the activities of others, as if it were the traditional superior-subordinate relationship. If team "leaders" act that way and send the message that the company doesn't really take this "team stuff" all that seriously, then other team members won't either.

The word "boss" has no place in teams. Bosses tell people what to do rather than facilitate cooperation and shared problem solving and decision making, which are at the heart of teamwork.

Not only should the team leader walk the walk and talk the talk, but the managers who act as sponsors for the team better do the same. If they do not put a high premium on teamwork and make sure the team has the resources and authority to do its work, the team will not come together.

Some things a team leader can do to be a good role model include:

- Look to the team for answers rather than giving the answers.

- Never blame an individual when something goes wrong. Look at the team's processes and work with team members to learn from the experience and improve processes so similar breakdowns are less likely to be repeated.

- Don't sit by while the team is doing various tasks on the way to achieving its objectives. The leader should have specific tasks to do just like all other team members. The leader is also a team member.

- Be ready to work with any team member who needs assistance. Do this from the perspective of a helper.

- Always share credit for team successes with the entire team.

- Communicate openly and honestly to encourage that kind of communication among all group members.

Leader Provides Vision

One way of thinking about a team leader is as a process owner. This means the person who, in the organization's hierarchy, is responsible for the management of some process. In this role, the team leader has the responsibility and opportunity to shape a vision for the team to provide direction for its efforts.

 A **vision** is a clearly articulated image for the future of a team or organization. It states where the team will be in the future and what it will have accomplished.

You can relate vision to team purpose and goals, but it goes beyond that. A vision is meant to inspire team members as to just how well they might succeed. It should not be unrealistic, but it should push people to go beyond ordinary performance. Some examples of vision statements might include:

- Our team will become the role model for teamwork in our company. (Sets a vision for and inspires cooperation among team members.)

- By cooperatively managing and improving processes, our team will decrease costs by half and reduce defects to less than 1%. (Sets a vision for performance that can come from teamwork.)

- In six months, our team will develop a new product that will be a hit in the market and we will plan this product for easy manufacturability and low cost. (A vision for a cross-functional product development team.)

Visions should help team members relate their ability to cooperate with what the team as a whole wants to achieve. With this vision in hand, the leader can then provide regular feedback on how the team is doing toward making this vision a reality. This type of feedback reinforces the team's motivation to move forward.

LEADER SELECTS TEAM MEMBERS

When a company decides to use a temporary team, such as a cross-functional project team, management will often select a person to be the team leader. This person then has the responsibility of selecting and recruiting people to be members of the team. Here are some steps for how to do this effectively:

- Think about potential members in terms of the team's objectives and purpose and the activities necessary to achieve these.

- Define the team jobs that need to be filled to execute the activities necessary to achieve goals.

- Identify people with the skills needed to fill the team jobs.

- Talk to potential candidates and find out their attitudes about working on teams and whether they would be good team players.

- Invite those people who have the skills and teamwork attitude to join the team.

 It's important for potential team members to have the skills needed, but it's equally or even more important to have the teamwork attitude. Otherwise, this member will potentially be a drag rather than a contributor to the team.

LEADER AS PROBLEM SOLVER

The leader is a resource for helping members solve problems, both of a technical and an interpersonal nature. As members run into roadblocks of one sort or another as they do their work, the leader is a person to whom they can turn to figure out how to deal with them.

 Being a resource to solve problems doesn't mean the leader is supposed to solve all team problems as they arise. When that happens, team members will depend on the leader rather than on the team as a whole to solve problems.

The idea of being a resource to the team is important in considering this responsibility of the leader. However, this does not mean the leader simply gives people the answer. Rather it means helping individuals and the team as a whole solve problems for themselves. Some problems a team might confront include the following:

- **A process breakdown where something happens that members don't anticipate.** The leader can call a meeting, explain the problem, and lead a brainstorming session to elicit ways to fix the breakdown.

- **A single team member is stuck on some task.** The leader can ask questions that will lead the member to consider the issues more fully. Or the leader might get others involved to help. Or the leader might share personal experiences in similar circumstances that this member can use. In each case, the leader doesn't necessarily solve the problem, but provides direction so the member can solve it.

- **A disagreement emerges between two team members that hinders their cooperation.** The leader can use a variety of approaches to help the members get their disagreement into the open and resolved.

 It's important that team members consider the leader to be a fair and impartial mediator of interpersonal problems, whose focus is on members cooperating to achieve goals. Otherwise, the leader will not have the respect necessary to help members resolve a personal disagreement.

LEADER AS LIAISON

The leader also serves as a liaison among other teams, team leaders, and management. In this role, the leader helps arrange the cooperation among teams and keeps management informed of team progress.

 A team that only focuses on its own goals rather than on how it fits in with other teams and the whole organization can end up working at cross purposes with those other teams. For example, a manufacturing team's search for product uniformity and efficiency ends up being a sales team's lack of product variety.

In addition to making sure the team's goals mesh with those of the organization, the leader must also coordinate with other teams so their actions don't become obstacles to the leader's team.

Three areas in which a team leader will take on the liaison role include:

- **Timing.** The outputs from any one team are usually the inputs needed by another team or group of people to do their work. They usually need these inputs at a certain time. Team leaders coordinate their actions with each other to minimize delays in delivery when needed and in the accumulation of work in progress.

Work in progress is partially completed work that is waiting in line for someone else to do something to it. Anytime there is work in progress, it costs the company money because it ties up resources and slows down delivery of final products to customers.

- **Turf Issues.** Sometimes it isn't clear which team is responsible for certain activities. A simple example might be who is supposed to load a truck—the team that gets outputs to the loading dock or the drivers? Team leaders, representing their teams, can usually work out such issues.

- **Resources.** Sometimes two teams need access to the same tools—for example, computers. Team captains can work out between them who might have access and when.

LEADERS TRAIN AND FACILITATE TRAINING

While it's not always true, a leader is often an expert in the technical areas in which the team works. As such, the leader may take on the responsibility of training people who need various skills or in setting up training with other team members or with outside trainers.

It may be the case that team members have responsibility for just one activity and have mastered this and want additional opportunities to learn and progress. In this case, the team leader should consider setting up cross-training programs. These give all team members the chance to learn the skills needed to do all the jobs the team is responsible for.

Cross-training involves training team members in all the skills involved in the various tasks and jobs the team is responsible for.

Cross-training gives team members the chance to expand their skills. Cross training also assures that should a team member be absent or should bottlenecks come up in certain steps of a process, other members can pitch in and do the work of that person or step.

In general, team leaders should focus on three types of training for team members:

- **Technical skills training.** This is training in actual job-related skills. Not only should the leader make sure everyone has this training, but it's a good idea to continuously schedule training that allows people to upgrade their skills and improve their methods.

- **Teamwork training.** This is training in various teamwork skills, including meetings, decision making, communication, and interpersonal relations. This facilitates the cooperation that is at the heart of teamwork.

- **Process management skills.** These are skills that help team members better understand the processes they are responsible for. Using such skills helps them prevent problems and waste from occurring, keep on schedule, minimize defective outputs, and continuously improve the overall operation of these processes.

LEADER AS CUSTOMER ADVOCATE

Team members intensely engaged in their tasks can sometimes forget about the needs of their customers, both internal and external. However, it is customers that give purpose to what the team does.

Acting as a customer advocate means the leader regularly reminds the team of the needs of their customers. As part of the liaison role, the leader should be checking regularly for feedback from customers. There are three types of customer feedback a leader should be concerned with:

- **Expressions of satisfaction with current outputs.** This lets the team know it's doing a good job. Often a leader doesn't receive feedback unless there is a problem. But it's a good idea to ask regularly about satisfaction even if no one is complaining. This provides assurance that processes are operating well and that the team is meeting customer needs.

- **Complaints.** When customers' expectations aren't being met, the leader is likely to receive complaints. These are very valuable because they provide direction for what needs to be improved. Quickly addressing complaints not only helps you improve your processes, but it also demonstrates the responsiveness that creates a strong bone between the team and its customers.

- **Suggestions for improvement.** A leader may also ask customers for ideas on how the team might improve its outputs to make them more useful. Those suggestions that the team can implement, it should implement. This again demonstrates responsiveness to customers.

The leader should regularly share this customer information with the team and be an advocate for the team continuously seeking to enhance customer satisfaction. As a role model, this activity will rub off on the team members and help assure that they all make customer satisfaction a high priority.

Any team member might take on the customer advocate role sometimes. If a team member has received customer feedback, he or she should share that with other team members. This reinforces the importance of customer satisfaction and helps improve the team's overall performance.

In this lesson, you learned the special tasks and roles of a team leader that contribute to the success of a team. In the next lesson, you will learn about self-directed teams.

SELF-DIRECTED TEAMS

In this lesson, you will learn what self-directed teams are all about and how organizations go about implementing this type of team.

At the Edy's Grand Ice Cream plant in Fort Wayne, Indiana, teams pretty much manage all operations. Team members deal with suppliers, hire new employees, and schedule production. Since going to self-directed teams, the company has seen scrap and rework as percentage of sales drop to 0.5%, which is an 83% reduction, in five years. It has seen a 57% increase in productivity and a 39% drop in costs. Saying that teams manage operations at Edy's means just that. There are essentially no middle managers or supervisors here. Team members working together make and implement all decisions with regard to operations. The point is: Done right, self-directed teams can make a big (and positive) difference in the success of an organization.

WHAT IS A SELF-DIRECTED TEAM?

A self-directed team is a team that doesn't have a manager. The team as a whole is responsible for everything that has to do with executing particular processes to deliver an output to either internal or external customers. When such teams are really humming, you can expect results such as described here for Edy's Grand Ice Cream. However, it takes time to get to that point, and in this lesson, we're going to review how organizations might go about developing high-performing, self-directed teams.

THE PATH TO SELF-DIRECTION

Managers don't decide one day to institute self-directed teams and overnight (or even over several months) have them in place. It's a slow process going from a model where managers and supervisors are considered responsible for processes to a model where teams have this responsibility.

In traditional organizations upper management can always blame some manager when a mistake happens. But with self-directed teams, there is no individual to blame. The team as a whole is accountable. But what they are most importantly accountable for is learning from the experience and improving their processes to make sure such mistakes don't happen again.

THE EVOLUTION OF A SELF-DIRECTED TEAM

There are five stages in the progress of a team from being leader-directed to being self-directed.

- **Stage 1.** The leader is responsible for the team from the perspective of management, but the team begins to handle day-to-day duties on their own. This is a stage that may last from startup to about six months into the team's evolution to becoming self-directed. (Adapted from "Self-Directed Teams Are Great, But They're Not Easy," *Journal for Quality and Participation*, Dec. 1993, pp. 64–70.)

- **Stage 2.** The team becomes more autonomous and has responsibility for planning, organizing, and executing work processes and mainly keeps the leader or manager informed of what they are doing. This is a stage that may run from months six to nine.

- **Stage 3.** The team takes full responsibility for organizing its work and for its productivity and the quality of its outputs. The supervisor may still be responsible for administrative decisions, such as vacations and other human resource issues. This stage lasts perhaps from months nine to 12.

- **Stage 4.** The team now has full responsibility for all its work, as well as working with suppliers and customers, with little contact with a supervisor or team leader. This stage may last from months 12 to 18.

- **Stage 5.** The team has taken over all functions involving its performance, including all administrative issues, such as hiring, rewards, and discipline. There is no leader specifically responsible for the team at this point. This is a fully functioning self-directed team. This stage may kick in at month 18 or later.

The team will never reach Stage 5 if the teamwork values we reviewed in Lesson 2 are not in place. Self-directed teams require a high level of trust and support by upper management. And they require time to develop into high-performing units.

INFORMATION SELF-DIRECTED TEAMS NEED TO PERFORM

The evolution through these stages toward becoming high-performing, self-directed teams requires that management share a substantial amount of information about strategy as well as operations with team members. The organization cannot expect a team to simply become the manager of itself without some understanding of what that involves and how to do it.

Like managers who are expected to perform well, the team has to be very clear about such items as:

- **The vision and mission of the organization, division, or department.** This means the team has to be very clear about how these different units understand what's expected of them and where the organization sees itself in the future. Further, the team has to know its specific role in achieving the mission and vision.

 The **vision** is a statement of how the organization sees itself in the future in terms of size, growth, achievements, recognition in the marketplace, and so on. (For example: We will have expanded our business as a gourmet fast food restaurant chain to every part of the state in five years.)

The **mission** describes what business the organization is in in terms of what benefits it delivers to customers. (For example: We provide our customers with carefully but quickly prepared gourmet lunches and dinners at prices just slightly higher than the hamburger joints.)

- **Department objectives.** The team needs to know the objectives of the department as set by top management, including schedules, timetables, and critical milestones that will indicate where the department stands in achieving these objectives.

- **Customers and suppliers.** The team must know who its customers are (whether they are internal or external) and what it takes to keep these customers satisfied. It must also know who its suppliers are and communicate with these suppliers about what the team needs from them to do its job well.

- **Budgeting issues.** The team should be aware of its budget and what's expected in terms of the effective management of this budget to achieve objectives.

It's important for teams to make their numerical objectives in terms of outputs and budgets, but it's equally important that the team not make meeting its "numbers" its primary goal. This can lead to manipulation of the system to look good. The purpose of goals for any team is to execute and improve its processes so it can profitably deliver outputs that meet and exceed customer expectations.

TRAINING FOR SELF-DIRECTION

The organization must make a strong commitment to training in several areas if it expects its teams to get to the point of performing at a level like those at Edy's Grand Ice Cream. There are four skill areas in which team members will require training:

- Teamwork

- Process management and problem-solving

- Administration

- Work and technical skills

In planning for such training, this is also the order in which the training should be delivered. In other words, start with the basics of teamwork, then process management and problem-solving, then administrative skills, and, on an ongoing basis, work skills. Let's look further at each of these.

 In general, teams should receive this training as they are ready for it and as management gives teams more responsibility and authority for operations. In other words, don't provide training in administrative activities, for example, until the team is getting ready to take those on.

TEAMWORK TRAINING

There are several skills involved in this area, many of which we have covered in this book. They include:

- How teams evolve into a performing unit (forming, storming, norming, performing) and what they can expect at each stage

- Team roles and who does what to keep the team operating smoothly
- Holding effective meetings and coming to consensus team decisions
- Communication skills that facilitate people working together well
- Resolving conflict among team members and among teams
- Effective coaching methods, so team members can help one another perform more effectively in their individual tasks and in cooperating with other members

An organization cannot expect a team to effectively cooperate if the members do not have skills such as these.

PROCESS MANAGEMENT AND PROBLEM-SOLVING TRAINING

Because teams are responsible, by definition, for executing processes, they need knowledge about the tools for doing this and how and when to use these tools. Training in these areas will include:

- Understanding and using tools for analyzing and measuring how well processes are operating
- Statistical process control and how to create and use control charts
- Methods for systematically improving process operation
- A problem-solving methodology that gets all team members involved to help one another

- Methods for anticipating problems and taking preventive actions, such as setting up and executing preventive maintenance schedules

- Methods for measuring customer satisfaction and what improvements might enhance customer satisfaction

ADMINISTRATIVE SKILLS TRAINING

This involves the work of planning, scheduling, hiring, purchasing, safety, and similar issues. Training includes:

- How to schedule work to efficiently use resources and meet customer requirements

- How to effectively select and hire new team members

- The budgeting process and how to develop an acceptable budget for the upcoming budgeting cycle

- How to develop and implement a safety plan

- Understanding financial performance documents and using them to evaluate performance and make decisions

- Understanding compensation issues and developing an equitable compensation plan

Self-directed teams may or may not have responsibility for compensation decisions, which may be controlled by management. However, the team can still make salary and bonus recommendations consistent with organizational policy.

WORK AND TECHNICAL SKILLS TRAINING

This involves training to upgrade job-related skills. It often will include training on new equipment or techniques. Cross-training will also be important. For the team to operate efficiently, all team member should have the skills and under-standing to do any of the tasks the team is responsible for.

 With self-directed teams, members often rotate jobs on a periodic basis to keep all members up to speed on all the team's skill areas. This also makes jobs more interesting as members are not doing the same tasks all the time.

A CONDITION FOR SELF-DIRECTED TEAM SUCCESS

Self-directed teams (or, indeed, teams in general) will most likely succeed when there is a good deal of interdependence required to complete a task. The team environment facilitates cooperation and communication so performance naturally improves. For example, members of a construction crew who must cooperate to get things done would, with proper train-ing, perform better when formally instituted as a team.

When teams don't seem to be working out, it's often because team members did not view their success as being dependent on what others do. If an organization tries to set up teams in this type of situation, employees will often see participating as a burden, taking up their time in nonproductive activities. An example might be a sales team where each member is responsible for a particular territory. In this case, the members might resent having to be on a team.

The fact is, however, that there is little work in an organization where people are not interdependent. If managers don't see this, it's usually because they have not properly analyzed their processes. By looking at processes, managers can find the interdependencies that exist among employees. And it is around these processes that teams should be set up.

Should the teams be self-directed? The answer is no, unless management is willing to commit to a long-term adoption of teamwork values and to invest in the required training. If top managers are willing to do this, then they can expect a continuously improving level of performance, decreased costs, and a high level of employee commitment and job satisfaction.

In this lesson, you learned what self-directed teams are all about and how organizations go about implementing this type of team. In the next lesson, you will learn about the role of communication in teamwork.

10

COMMUNICATION FOR TEAMWORK

In this lesson, you will learn how communication takes place, how team members might misunderstand one another, and some communication techniques that facilitate cooperation, efficiency, and commitment among team members.

In Lesson 2, you learned that one of the values of teamwork is open, honest communication. Now we're going to learn about some communication techniques based on this value. Communication is vital to teams. It's the lubricant that facilitates cooperation. If team members don't communicate openly and honestly, cooperation will be severely compromised. And if you compromise cooperation, team performance suffers.

Communication in the context of teams is the process of transmitting and understanding information and ideas—as well as feelings and emotions—to influence behavior and cooperation.

HOARDING AND SHARING INFORMATION

In organizations where people don't fully appreciate the value of teams, managers will hoard information and be secretive in their communications. They equate access to information with power. Then when things go wrong and these managers ask "why?", the response they can expect to this question is "I didn't know."

But in organizations where managers appreciate the importance of the systems view and the value of teams in executing processes, it's just the opposite. They know that open communication and sharing of information is necessary for people to collaborate in an intelligent and informed manner—vital if you want to eliminate mistakes that come from people "not knowing."

 Open communication and information sharing help team members anticipate what they can expect from one another and when they can expect it. Open communication eliminates surprises and makes it easy for members to work together.

A BASIC PRINCIPLE OF COMMUNICATION

Before we review how communication happens, here's a basic principle you should always remember:

You can't not communicate.

Yes, the double negative is intentional. Everything you say and do, or don't say and don't do, imparts meaning to others. You can't escape that. They will put some interpretation on everything that happens. Knowing that, you want to make sure that the way they interpret your words and actions, or silence and inaction, are consistent with what you wanted. You want there to be the shared understanding that makes it possible for your team to work together to successfully execute and improve its processes.

 Shared understanding means that the person who sent the message and the person who received it interpret it and the actions it implies in the same way. Without shared understanding, team members can make incorrect assumptions about what someone else means or is doing and compromise process efficiency.

THE COMMUNICATION PROCESS

People who study communication have developed a model for describing how it occurs. Understanding this model is useful to team members because it reminds them of how communication happens and how it can break down and how members might come to misunderstand one another. Figure 10.1 shows this model, which we're going to review in a little more detail.

- **Step 1. Sender encodes message.** Let's say you're a team leader and you want to deliver a message to a team member. To do that, you compose or create your message using symbols, usually words, sometimes images, along with nonverbal signals, designed to convey what you have in mind. The potential for misunderstanding starts here. For example, if team members aren't familiar with the words and images you've selected, your message is subject to incorrect interpretation as they try to figure out what you mean.

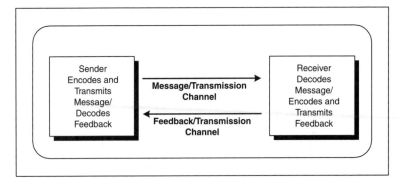

Figure 10.1   How communication works.

- **Step 2. Sender transmits the message by some channel.** These channels might be, for example, face-to-face conversation, telephone, e-mail, voice mail, letter, memo, video conference, and so on. It's important to select a channel that's appropriate for the message. Some channels are more conducive to feedback and some less. Less possibility for feedback introduces more possibility for misunderstanding because receivers can't easily check whether they have correctly interpreted what you meant to say.

A **communication channel** is the means by which a sender transmits a message. The face-to-face channel allows for the most interaction between sender and receiver and an impersonal memo the least.

- **Step 3. Receiver decodes message.** This means the receiver, for example, another team member, translates or interprets the message. Receivers will always do this according to their personal knowledge and experience. If the sender and receiver have different backgrounds, assumptions, skills, knowledge, and experience, there is a good chance the receiver will decode the message differently from the sender's intent.

- **Step 4. Receiver transmits feedback and sender decodes it.** If the channel makes it possible and feedback is appropriate, the receiver will tell the sender what he or she has heard, again using symbols, such as words and images. This gives the recipient the chance to ask for clarification and make comments that refine the original message. In other words, it allows both sender and receiver to interact to improve on the possibility that there is shared understanding between them. We can say that when feedback occurs, we have two-way communication going on.

Two-way communication means both parties have the opportunity to express ideas, listen, and respond to one another to bring about shared understanding and cooperation.

THE HEART OF COMMUNICATION

The fundamental goal of communication on teams is shared understanding to bring about cooperation. Here are the two components of communication that make that happen:

- **Listening.** It's the only way you can find out what someone else is thinking and wants to do.

- **Giving feedback.** It's the only way you can make sure you understand the person and your specific response to his or her ideas.

Let's look at each of these and how they make a difference in communicating for teamwork.

THE IMPORTANCE OF LISTENING

A reason why shared understanding doesn't happen when people communicate is because individuals *listen to respond rather than listen to understand.* This means they search for information that will allow them to deal with a situation quickly rather than correctly. They pick up a few cues from the discussion and then formulate a response that's consistent with their viewpoint while not taking into account the viewpoint of the speaker. In other words, people listen to answer rather than to understand and, predictably, end up often misunderstanding one another. (This idea is explained in detail in *The 7 Habits of Highly Effective People,* New York: Fireside Books, 1989. Habit 5 is "Seek first to understand and then to be understood.")

ACTIVE LISTENING

The opposite of this type of listening is what we can call active listening. This involves taking conscientious actions to understand the message another person is sending from his or her perspective.

Why is active listening important? Because the only way team members can know what other members know is to listen to them. Active listening is a way to do that. If team members don't practice active listening:

- They close themselves off to what these other members have to offer.

- They close themselves off to effective collaboration.

- They open the door to mistaken assumptions about what they thought other members had in mind because they didn't listen closely.

- They create an environment in which other team members will also fail to practice active listening.

Here are some characteristics of team members who practice active listening:

- Active listeners pay attention to the whole of the sender's message, without interruption or jumping to conclusions.

- Active listeners continuously seek to interpret the sender's message from the perspective of the sender by checking to make sure they are interpreting the message correctly.

Here are some practical tactics you as a team member can use to improve your active listening skills:

- **Stop working on anything else while meeting with another team member.** Working while trying to listen will be a distraction and prevents you from focusing on the intended message of the sender.

- **Use nonverbal cues to show the sender that you are interested.** Show your interest in the ideas of the sender by leaning toward him or her, smiling, and nodding in a natural way.

- **Pay close attention to the speaker's non-verbal behavior.** Attempt to determine the individual's emotional state. (For example: Is the person angry, hurt, indifferent, or enthusiastic?)

- **Use probes and paraphrases to clarify the sender's intended message.** Active listeners paraphrase the sender's message to make sure they understand it. By putting the sender's ideas in your own words, you provide a test that you have accurately decoded the message.

- **Ask open-ended questions that allow the speaker to explain his or her position in more detail.** Open-ended questions also show that the listener is not defensive and is willing to consider an alternative position.

- **Close conversations with a summary statement.** This provides a synopsis of the speaker's main ideas and provides the speaker with an opportunity to clarify the intended message.

- **Find time to listen.** Active listeners have a good *talk-listen ratio.* If you are talking more than 50 percent of the time, you are probably not adequately listening to other team members.

The **talk-listen ratio** is the percent of time that you talk during a conversation compared to the amount of time you listen.

Facilitating cooperation requires active listening. And the bonus in all this is that by listening to others, you create an environment where they will want to listen to you as well.

Active listening and the other points raised in this lesson are appropriate both for one-on-one communication and for communication in groups or in team meetings.

FEEDBACK

If you want to make sure you understand what somebody else means, give the speaker feedback that says "This is what I think you mean. Am I correct?" This gives the person a chance to clarify any points that aren't clear. The point in giving feedback is always to help both parties come to shared understanding. If done improperly, however, it can generate arguments and all kinds of defensive behaviors. These undermine teamwork and compromise, and, sometimes substantially, team performance.

Here are some feedback techniques that will assure that there is shared understanding among team members and that those communicating have explored an issue completely, and that they are carefully listening to one another.

- **Make feedback specific as to what, when, where, and so on.** Generalizations prolong the time needed to make sure the person delivering the feedback understands. "So we should begin this project on April 8, right?"

- **Be nonjudgmental in asking questions or making comments.** This encourages further clarification in an open manner. "You believe that this new product would appeal to boomers?"

- **Always focus on behaviors and actions and not the personality of the speaker.** Behaviors can be clarified without the speaker becoming defensive. "You're saying you will purchase all the supplies we need?"

- **Express disagreements precisely.** In this way, speakers can either further explain their ideas or change them. "It's not a good idea to spend money on a new computer because this job doesn't require one."

- **If you are enthusiastic, act that way.** Enthusiasm helps build commitment to take actions together. "That's great! What are our next steps?"

 During meetings, feedback techniques are useful for leaders and other team members to keep discussions going and for making sure points are clearly made and understood by all team members.

Communication and Commitment

When individuals feel they are being listened to and understood and that others respect what they have to say, this engenders a similar feeling in return. This is another way of saying that people feel committed to others when they feel others are committed to them. In other words, open communication and information sharing go hand in hand with commitment to the team and its objectives. And such commitment contributes to the cooperation that is at the heart of effective teamwork.

Commitment comes from a personal identification with an organization and its purpose, and causes people to want to take actions to help the organization succeed. People feel this way when they believe the organization has their best interests at heart as well.

In this lesson, you learned how communication takes place, how team members might misunderstand one another, and some communication techniques that facilitate cooperation, efficiency, and commitment among team members. In the next lesson, you will learn about dealing with conflict on teams.

11

Dealing with Conflict on Teams

In this lesson, you will learn how to understand the sources of team conflicts and how to resolve conflicts in a win-win manner.

Jose tells Cynthia he needs certain data from her by Tuesday at noon for a report he's preparing for the team. Cynthia believes this means Jose really needs them by Wednesday, and so she feels no sense of urgency to deliver before Wednesday. When Cynthia doesn't give him the information he needs on Tuesday, Jose accuses her of ignoring his request. Cynthia replies she didn't believe it was that important, and an argument ensues. Perhaps this is just the latest in a series of misunderstandings between Jose and Cynthia. What we have is here is a conflict.

A **conflict** is a disagreement about time, procedures, or goals, or a combination of these. Conflicts are a concern because they get in the way of team members collaborating with each other to execute their processes.

Conflicts on a team usually result from a mismatch of expectations among team members. In other words, when two or more team members have different perspectives on a situation, what they expect of each other, and what should happen, the result can be a conflict.

Conflicts also arise because of unintentional miscommunication and misunderstandings among team members. Whatever the reason, conflicts cause members to work at cross purposes with one another. And conflicts usually interfere with work altogether as members spend time bickering with one another rather than doing their jobs.

 Conflicts are usually a symptom that a team is not well focused and that communication is not as open and complete as it should be. In this sense, the team can view a conflict as an opportunity to learn and make improvements that will prevent similar conflicts from happening in the future.

DIFFERENT TYPES OF CONFLICTS

The mismatches of expectations that are at the base of conflict mainly take two forms—interpersonal conflict and conflict between teams.

INTERPERSONAL CONFLICT

The first type of conflict is interpersonal conflict. Just as the names implies, this is a disagreement between two or more individuals. It could be between team members, between a team member and the team leader, or between individuals on different teams.

There are many causes of conflicts between individuals on teams, and you'll learn about several of them in this lesson. One example comes from misunderstandings about who is supposed to do what task and when it's supposed to be done— the Jose and Cynthia type conflict in the previous example.

Conflict Between Teams

Conflict between teams represents disagreements between teams whose processes depend on one another but whose goals may be different. Common conflicts of this nature might occur between the sales team and a manufacturing team. The sales team seeks to sell just what customers want. The manufacturing team wants to simplify production and minimize variety. Another example might come from a planning team wanting certain data from a line team, such as in warehousing, the collecting of which this team believes distracts them from doing their normal work.

Specific Causes of Conflict

Let's start from the idea that mismatches of expectations are at the base of team conflicts. However, there are a number of different reasons why team members have conflicting expectations of each other. By identifying the actual cause of a particular conflict, team members can more effectively eliminate that as a disrupting element in the smooth running of the team and its processes.

Scarce Resources

Resources needed to do work include money, supplies, information, and tools. In organizations where team members feel they must compete for these or where there is no provision for the equitable sharing of what is available, conflict either among team members or between teams is a possibility.

For example, one resource that could be a cause of conflicts might be computers. These are useful for many activities, yet there are often not enough for all team members to have access whenever they want. Members may argue over who needs the computer the most at any point in time. Similar disagreements can ensue over budget allocations or any scarce resource.

POOR COMMUNICATION

The inability to communicate in a way that leads team members or teams to come to shared understanding often leads to conflict. In fact, this might be the most common cause of conflict. Miscommunication can occur, for example, when two team members have different cultural backgrounds. Or perhaps one team member is insensitive to others and may interrupt and make sarcastic remarks that offend another member of the team. This leads to the two refusing to work together and job disruption. Poor communication is one of the most common causes of conflicts.

AMBIGUITIES ABOUT RESPONSIBILITY

Ambiguities about responsibility means that it's unclear who is responsible for completing certain tasks. When this occurs, the team members involved will either argue about who should have done these tasks when they don't get done or about who should be doing them.

For example, a conflict could arise between a team member in any department and a team member who works in the mail room about who was supposed to get an urgent letter out that didn't get sent on time. It may be unclear who takes care of such situations, and this can lead to a conflict. The resolution, of course, is eliminating the ambiguity by either setting up a procedure or encouraging communication to deal with special situations.

INCOMPATIBLE GOALS

When different individuals or departments have goals that are not coordinated with one another, they have incompatible goals. Such goals can cause team members or different teams to work at cross purposes with one another. This incompatibility often involves spending extra time or money to do a job as well as possible or deliver to customers exactly what they want versus the need to keep costs down. For example, a team member may want a special tool that costs $500 that will enhance his or her performance, and the team leader decides to turn this down because this tool is not in the budget. The result can be a conflict.

PERSONALITY DIFFERENCES

Personality differences involve mismatches in the way people expect each other to behave and interact on a personal level. People of one personality type just don't get along with people of different personality types. Extroverts can irritate introverts, for example.

Often personality differences have less to do with individual personality characteristics than with personal insecurities. An insecure person is often likely to feel that an outgoing and confident employee is a threat, resulting in arguments and poor cooperation between these individuals. For example, a person who knows his skills are lacking may put on an aggressive front to hide this inadequacy, provoking conflicts with fellow employees.

In helping employees deal with this type of conflict, you have to look beyond just the subject matter of the disagreement and get to the root cause. You may never get two people to like one another, but you can reach a state where they will work together in a collaborative manner.

Resolving Conflicts

The most important way to resolve conflicts is to prevent them. If team members and the team leader can take actions to share information and encourage teamwork and genuine cooperation among the members of the team and throughout the organization, they are taking actions that will prevent conflict. Yet when conflicts do pop up, as they undoubtedly will (because we can never anticipate all the problems that are likely to occur among people), the team needs to know how to intelligently resolve these.

The teamwork values reviewed in Lesson 2 can go a long way in helping teams prevent conflict. These values are based on team members understanding that their personal success is tied to helping other team members succeed.

There are several approaches team members can take to resolve conflicts. The goal in doing this is to create a situation where the expectations of all employees and departments are aligned with each other. Another goal is to make sure that these expectations and understandings are consistent with the objectives of process improvement and customer satisfaction.

Win-Win Conflict Resolution

In thinking about resolving conflict, remember that the best approach the team can take is one that emphasizes a win-win resolution for everyone. If the team finds that it has to use an approach that moves away from win-win, it will be less likely that members will solve the conflict permanently.

 Win-win resolution means that all parties in a conflict feel good about the resolution, and there is no sense that one party has won and another has lost.

Methods Teams Use to Resolve Conflicts

There is a variety of ways that conflicts can get resolved on teams. These range from situations where both parties feel they have to give up something to resolve the problem to situations where both parties feel they have gained from the resolution.

The former often deals with symptoms of conflict, getting people to change their behaviors without getting at what motivated the misunderstanding in the first place. The latter gets at the source of the problem and helps people understand what drives their differences and ultimately get beyond those to a common ground. It's what every team should seek, but let's look at the other methods as well.

COMPROMISE

In the compromise approach to resolution, the team leader or another member talks to both parties with the goal of having each one give in a little on their position, trying to find a middle ground that both can live with. It's useful to use compromise when both parties think they are right but are willing to listen to the other person.

 In shaping a compromise, the team leader may talk to each member separately at first to understand the mismatch of expectations, and then bring the two members together to work out the compromise.

With compromise, both parties will feel they have given up something to gain resolution. Compromise will usually end a conflict for the time being, but it can leave remnants of resentment that may result in more conflict in the future.

MEDIATION

Mediation is similar to compromise except that it is conducted by an impartial third person who has the authority to make the final decision on the resolution. This approach might be used when there is a conflict between a team member and the team leader or between members of different teams.

The mediator tries to work out a solution acceptable to both parties. However, if that's not possible, the mediator will suggest or impose a solution that both parties agree to abide by. Such resolutions work at the time, but they also can leave lingering resentments that can cause the conflict to reoccur.

WHY COMPROMISE AND MEDIATION DON'T ALWAYS WORK

The reason compromise and mediation often don't permanently resolve a conflict is because they don't change people's assumptions that underlie their disagreement. When people have different assumptions, they will behave in ways that can result in conflict. If these individuals cannot come to agreement on their assumptions, they will not permanently resolve their conflicts.

Assumptions represent people's understanding about how a process is supposed to work and what their role is in that process. Assumptions drive people's behavior. A mismatch of expectations is really a mismatch of assumptions.

THE BEST APPROACH TO CONFLICT RESOLUTION

The best approach to resolving conflicts is what we might call *collaborative dialog*. This is an approach that gets conflicting team members or teams looking at their assumptions and behaviors in light of their individual, team, and organizational goals.

A **dialog** is the process of two or more people exploring the assumptions they use as individuals to understand situations and decide what to do. The goal of dialog is to come to shared assumptions that drive cooperation and teamwork.

Coming to understand the assumptions that lead to the mismatching of expectations and how these mismatches affect team performance is key to permanently resolving conflict. It is also key to helping people grow and work together in an ever more committed fashion.

Collaborative dialog is the best approach to resolving conflict because it not only puts the conflict behind people, it can also result in improved methods of working together. It is the only way to get to the win-win approach for all concerned.

One way to facilitate an examination of assumptions is to get each person or team to take the other party's side. This helps both sides to understand where the other is coming from.

SOME WAYS TO FACILITATE COLLABORATIVE DIALOG

With collaborative dialog, the team gets away from people defending their points of view and toward understanding one another so they work together efficiently and effectively.

"I" MESSAGES

One way to facilitate the dialog that leads to shared assumptions is for both parties to explain their positions using "I" messages, not "you" messages. This keeps both parties focused on taking responsibility for their feelings and behaviors instead of blaming the other person for these. For example:

- "**I** believe that the first step in the process should be to..." rather than "**You** are supposed to do this at this point..."

- "**I** felt I was supposed to know how to do that task even though I was unsure of the procedure" rather than "**You** didn't do what you're supposed to do, so I was unsure of what to do next."

"You" statements put people on the defensive. "I" statements let others know what an individual assumes and understands.

BE NONJUDGMENTAL

Another way to help get at assumptions and bring about dialog is to avoid making judgmental statements, either about yourself or others. For example, do say "Here's my concern about this situation." Don't say, "It's stupid to assume that..." or "This person doesn't know up from down." Judgments bring out defensive behaviors that prolong the conflict. Nonjudgmental statements get at what's actually going on, so everyone can understand the situation better, learn from the experience, and make changes that result in cooperation and improvement.

In this lesson, you learned how to understand the sources of team conflicts and how to resolve conflicts in a win-win manner. In the next lesson, you will learn about four tools for managing team processes.

12

PROCESS MANAGEMENT TOOLS FOR TEAMS, PART 1

In this lesson, you will learn about four basic tools for effectively managing and improving the processes for which the team is responsible.

In Lesson 1, we learned that the reason for implementing teams is that they facilitate the cooperation necessary to execute work processes. Cooperation based on teamwork values such as reviewed in Lesson 2 is necessary, but to effectively manage and improve work processes, teams need to use various process management tools. These tools help team members:

- Understand the process and its steps

- Execute process steps in an error-free manner

- Determine how well the process is operating

- Provide methods for making process improvements

In this lesson and the next, we're going to review some tools that help teams operate in an efficient manner and deliver outputs that meet customer needs.

FLOWCHARTS

Flowcharts are diagrams that show the steps involved in executing a process. They are like maps that show the sequence of activities and tasks by which some input is transformed into an output for a customer. Figure 12.1 shows a basic flowchart for the process involved in changing the oil in a car.

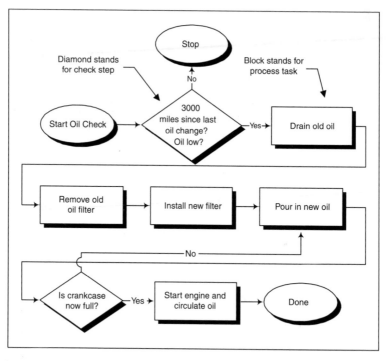

Figure 12.1   A simple flowchart showing the steps in the oil change process.

Flowcharts are one of the most important tools a team can use to understand and begin to get control of the processes it's responsible for. Many times when a team is just starting out, an early activity is mapping out their process steps using a flowchart.

Often doing this becomes a real learning experience. Team members may find that the process is more complicated than they thought. Having the flowchart helps them identify steps that are unnecessary or redundant with other steps. The team can take actions to eliminate those steps.

They also often find that there are several steps included to fix mistakes that happened somewhere else in the process. Such steps are indicated by the diamond check steps shown in Figure 12.1. The step usually says something like this: "Does output meet specifications?" If not, it goes to the "fix it" part of the process. If it does meet specifications, it continues to move ahead toward completion.

 All the diamonds and "fix it" steps in a flowchart represent opportunities for process improvements. By taking actions to eliminate whatever causes an output to be defective, you eliminate the need for repair or scraping of such outputs. This means the process operates more efficiently and the overall quality of outputs is increased—good for the team and company and good for customers.

The team can build a process flowchart by taking the process apart and identifying each task that must be done through time to deliver a final acceptable output. For a complicated process, the team might want to break down into subgroups, with each responsible for analyzing a subprocess. Once team members agree on how their process currently operates, they can use the flowchart as a starting point for figuring out how to make improvements.

A **subprocess** is a series of steps or tasks that make up a part of a larger process. For example, a subprocess for an accounting team might include collecting current financial data. Such data are then used to update accounts, which is another subprocess.

 In figuring out the steps in a process, an effective method is for team members to write the specific tasks on sticky notes and then arrange these on a wall or whiteboard. This method allows them to explore what's actually involved and organize them in an order that everyone agrees on.

CHECKLISTS

Sometimes it's helpful for a complicated process or one in which precision or safety are concerns to have a checklist of steps to help assure that all the tasks in executing a process step or steps are done properly. If that's the case, the team can develop checklists that serve as reminders for what must be done, and in what order. Then when an activity is completed, the checklists document that all the tasks involved have been properly completed. Such lists can be valuable to team members when there is a problem at some point downstream in the process, and they are trying to identify potential causes.

An example of a checklist would be for mixing a batch of chemicals for use in an industrial process. Such an activity requires specific steps to be followed and a checklist helps assure these happen as they are supposed to.

A **checklist** is a list of specific tasks that must be completed to execute a process step. It includes a place to check off that each task has been completed.

Figure 12.2 shows a checklist for completion of this book. While this is really a kind of To Do list for a single project, checklists as process management tools serve as permanent To Do lists, serving as a prop to make sure what's supposed to happen does happen.

CHECKLIST FOR PREPARATION OF MANUSCRIPT

TASKS	Done
Step 1. Determine content for each chapter	✓
Step 2. Write draft of each chapter	✓
Step 3. Prepare figures for chapters	✓
Step 4. Revise draft, adding sidebars	✓
Step 5. Have chapters reviewed	
Step 6. Revise Manuscript	
Step 7. Deliver Manuscript to Publisher	

Figure 12.2   A standard checklist. As each task is completed, the user checks it off.

CHECKSHEETS

If the team wants to collect data about how a process is operating, the members can create checksheets to do this. This is a tool that allows a team member to keep accurate counts of, for example, different types of defects, problems, how many items are completed per hour, or anything the team would like to have counts of. They can then use this data to understand how well a process is operating or to anticipate and handle problems of various sorts.

 A **checksheet** is a tool for counting the number of some item in which you have an interest. It helps answer questions like "how many" and "how often."

If you run a fast food restaurant, for example, you could develop a checksheet to keep track of how many of each type of sandwich are ordered during lunch. Having this information is valuable for making sure you have enough ingredients to match demand.

Another use of a checksheet might be in a customer service call-in department. The checksheet can help you keep track of how many calls you receive at different hours of the day as well as what types of questions customers are asking. With such data in hand, you can then use this to help schedule reps and make it easier and quicker to deal with common problems.

Figure 12.3 shows a checksheet developed by a motorpool team for keeping a count of various types of repairs. Having this data can help the team know what kinds of problems to anticipate and refine its processes for effectively handling them.

CAR R   CAR REPAIR CHECKSHEET

PROBLEM	JAN	FEB	MAR	APR	TOTALS
Clutch Slippage	HH	HH II	HH	HH III	25
Brakes	HHHH	HHHHI	HHHHHI	HH II	39
Radiator Leaks	HH III	HH I	HH	HH IIII	27
Air Conditioner Problems	HHIIII	HH II	HH II	HHHH	33
Oil Leaks	HHHH	HHHH	HHHH	HH IIII	39

Figure 12.3 A checksheet used to count various events or attributes, in this case car repairs.

PARETO CHARTS

Perhaps you have heard the saying that 80% of problems are created by 20% of possible causes. So if you can deal with those 20% of causes you can eliminate the majority of your problems. The Pareto chart is a tool to help you track and identify that 20% of causes.

It's named after a 19th century Italian economist, Vilfredo Pareto, who studied the distribution of wealth and determined that the most of the wealth was concentrated in a few families while the great majority of people were poor. Joseph Juran, a well-known management consultant, rediscovered this idea and generalized it to take in any kind of 80-20 type situation. Juran refers to the significant 20% as the "vital few" and to the remaining 80% as the "trivial many," and that's a good way to think about them.

The value of the Pareto chart is that it graphically displays which vital few you should be concerned with. Figure 12.4 shows a Pareto chart for different types of defects of a process. Having this information, the team may be able to determine which activities in the process might be responsible for these defects. Then members can make changes that result in substantial improvement very quickly.

In reality, the 80-20 rule is not absolute. Team members might find, for example, that two kinds of causes are responsible for 65% of their problems or 25% of customers take 60% of their outputs. The point is that by dealing with the vital few, team members can quickly take actions that keep processes working efficiently or keep those customers happy.

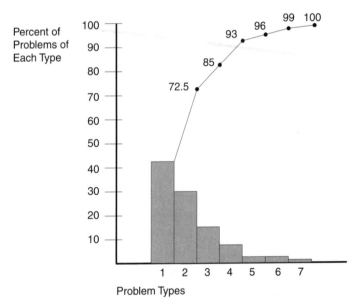

Figure 12.4   A typical Pareto chart showing that most problems are of a similar nature or the result of one or two causes. In this figure, dealing with the causes of problems 1 and 2 takes care of 72.5% of all problems.

In this lesson, you learned about four basic tools for effectively managing and improving the processes for which the team is responsible. In the next lesson, you will learn about four more process management tools.

13

PROCESS MANAGEMENT TOOLS FOR TEAMS, PART 2

In this lesson, you will learn about four more basic tools for effectively managing and improving the processes for which the team is responsible.

If we think of cooperation and teamwork values as the heart of process management, then we can think of the tools we are reviewing here and in the last lesson as its mind. By intelligently using these tools, a team will be able to measure how well it's doing, and make fact-based decisions to improve.

CAUSE AND EFFECT DIAGRAMS

What happens at any step in a process is a confluence of causes from which we get some effect. For example, if a company is late in delivering a piece of equipment to a customer and wants to understand why, it can use a cause and effect diagram to do this.

Usually this tool is used in team meetings. An agenda item might be to identify the causes of some problem. The team might then brainstorm what the various causes might be and develop a cause and effect diagram as a way to see what these causes are, how they relate to one another, and how to address them.

 A **cause and effect diagram** is a graphical device for identifying causes that bring about a particular effect or outcome. By effectively managing causes, you can assure that the outcome you want will happen.

A cause and effect diagram is also called a "fishbone diagram" because of its appearance. It consists of a long "spine" that points to the effect with "bones" coming off of it that represent potential causes. There are generally five generic causes that you can associate with most processes:

- **People.** This includes concerns about training, management, communication, scheduling, and so on.

- **Measurement.** These are concerns about proper measurements, adjustments, and measuring devices.

- **Materials.** This includes concerns about using the right materials, parts, ingredients, and so on.

- **Equipment.** These are concerns about the equipment used, its maintenance, and availability.

- **Methods.** This includes concerns about the ways people do various tasks and interact to perform various activities.

A cause and effect diagram doesn't have to use these five generic causes. You can use whatever seems appropriate to the situation, but these work for most problems. Figure 13.1 shows a typical cause and effect diagram for a late delivery problem using these five generic causes

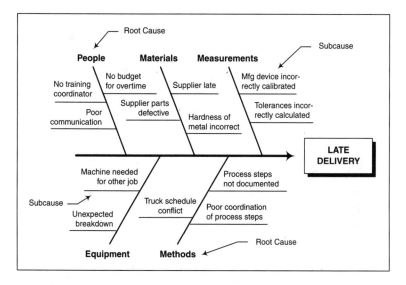

Figure 13.1   A cause and effect diagram. The lines coming from the spine are root causes and the smaller lines are subcauses.

 This tool will usually show that a particular effect happens because of multiple causes—some easy to deal with, some difficult. If you want the system and its processes your dealing with to work well, you need to address all the causes that bring about an effect. Start with the easy ones and work through them all.

In addition to using this tool to identify the causes of problems, you can also use it to plan how to bring about desirable effects or outcomes. Start with the outcome you would like and then identify all the causes or behaviors that will bring about that outcome.

FIVE WHYS

The cause and effect diagram is a way to identify a combination of causes for a particular output or effect. However, let's say you are dealing with a smaller problem somewhere in the midst of your processes. The five whys is a good way for the team to get to the root cause of that problem.

In traditional approaches to problem solving, managers often look at a some problem and do something to alleviate its apparent cause. In fact, what they are doing is dealing with a *symptom* of a problem that lies somewhere deeper in the system. Dealing with symptoms rather than causes does not solve a problem; it just hides it temporarily.

A **root cause** is the primary cause of a problem that may only become apparent several steps later in a process.

The actual principle here is less tied to the number of times you ask "why" than to your asking it enough times to discover the actual cause of a particular problem. We must resist the temptation to accept the path of least resistance and accept the first reasonable or plausible answer. Taiichi Ohno, former Toyota Motor vice president, provides the following example of finding the real cause of a machine stoppage. (Taiichi Ohno, *Toyota Production System: Beyond Large-Scale Production*, Cambridge, MA: Productivity Press, 1988, p. 17.)

First Why: Why did the machine stop?

First Answer: There was an overload and the fuse blew.

Second Why: Why was there an overload?

Second Answer: The bearing was not sufficiently lubricated.

Third Why: Why was it not lubricated sufficiently?

Third Answer: The lubrication pump was not pumping sufficiently.

Fourth Why: Why was it not pumping sufficiently?

Fourth Answer: The shaft of the pump was worn and rattling.

Fifth Why: Why was the shaft worn out?

Fifth Answer: There was no strainer attached and metal scrap got in.

By repeating why at least five times, the team can identify the real cause and hence the real solution: attaching a strainer to the lubricating pump. If team members had not carried out the questioning, they might have settled with an intermediate and plausible solution, such as replacing the fuse. But this would not have gotten at the root cause, and the problem would reappear. Asking why over and over uncovers the problem's cause deep in the system, a cause that is often hidden behind more obvious symptoms.

Many times managers are tempted to ask "Who?" when a problem occurs, as in "Who messed up?" This is nearly always the wrong question. The right question is "What about our processes is bringing about this problem?" One way to answer that question is to ask why at least five times.

HISTOGRAMS

Let's say the team asks a question about how well a process is operating and the amount of variation in the outputs of that process. A histogram is a way to graphically capture data that helps answer this question. This tool is especially valuable to show the frequency of occurrence of outputs of different continuous measures, such as weight, height, thickness, and time.

A **histogram** is a kind of bar chart that illustrates how often or frequently outputs of different measures emerge from a process.

The histogram can you show you which measurement happens most often, how wide the variation is in your outputs, and whether the variation takes the shape of a standard distribution (a "bell shaped curve") or if something unusual is going on that gives the outputs some other type distribution. Figure 13.2 shows a histogram that shows the frequency of steel shafts of different lengths from a manufacturing process.

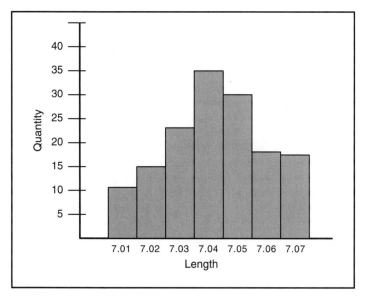

Figure 13.2   A histogram showing the quantity of outputs of different lengths.

   Variation means how much and how often outputs differ from one another and from a specification or target measure for the outputs. There is always variation in a process, but an important team goal is to reduce it to a level where it does not affect the quality of the output.

Using the information from a histogram, a team can learn how well its processes are operating and begin to make decisions for how to improve the operations of its processes.

THE PDCA IMPROVEMENT CYCLE

This isn't exactly a tool, but a way to use the tools we have been reviewing in this lesson and Lesson 12. It is the Plan, Do, Check, Act (PDCA) cycle for disciplined process improvement.

 The **PDCA Cycle** is a set of steps to follow for a team to continuously improve its processes. By making PDCA an important part of the team's responsibilities, the team helps assure that its processes will be more efficient and that its outputs will be less costly and higher quality.

In using this approach to improvement, teams do the following:

- Gather information about a process and *plan* changes they think will improve its operation.

- Implement or *do* the plan.

- *Check* whether the change represents an improvement and how well the process now operates.

- Make any final changes based on the check step, and *act* on what you find out to make the change permanent.

- Then repeat this planning procedure continuously— seeking ever more efficiency and higher quality outputs.

The PDCA cycle may not be new to you. It's essentially what people do anytime they try a new way to do something: they plan what they want to do; they try or implement the change;

they see how well it works; and they make further changes based on how well things went. It's how we learn. PDCA simply institutionalizes this idea so organizations can keep improving what they do. As shown in Figure 13.5 the cycle goes uphill, indicating you are continuously reaching for higher levels of performance.

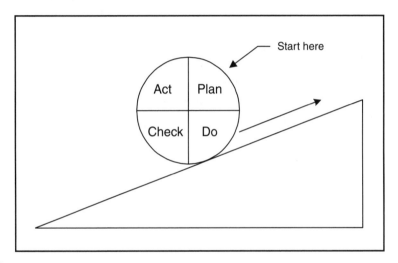

Figure 13.5   The PDCA cycle for continuous process improvement.

 The reason we call PDCA a *cycle* is because it is never ending. No matter how well a process is operating, it can always be improved using new techniques and technology.

If an improvement requires costly new technology, it may be more expensive to implement than it's worth. The team's goal with improvements is to make processes operate more efficiently so it can deliver higher value for customers at a lower price, not a higher price.

In this lesson, you learned about four more basic tools and techniques for effectively managing and improving the processes for which the team is responsible. In the next lesson, you will learn about one more important process management tool, control charts.

14

A TEAM PROBLEM SOLVING PROCESS

In this lesson, you will learn a 7-step method that teams can use to understand and solve process problems.

In any work situation, there are going to be problems. There's always going be an element of unpredictability in any activity in which we are engaged that can cause unexpected problems that affect the efficiency of a process or the quality of outputs or both.

A **problem** represents a situation in which actual conditions differ from what's desired and gets in the way of performance or when a quesion arises to which the team needs an answer to proceed effectively with its tasks.

When problems occur, the team needs a way to address and solve these problems. Throughout the lessons in this book you've seen an emphasis on the importance of the team understanding and effectively managing processes. The same is true for solving problems. The team needs a sound process for solving problems as they occur. What follows in this lesson is such a process. By following this process in a disciplined manner, the team can efficiently solve problems as they arise and get on with its work.

Not all problems need to be addressed using the formal problem solving process described here. Many times, small problems arise that a team member can promptly address alone. But when problems occur that will affect other team members and when there is no clear-cut course of action, then the formal problem-solving process is appropriate.

THE PROBLEM-SOLVING PROCESS

Many times people consider problem solving to just be the action an individual or team takes to take care of a situation. The fact is that action is important, and understanding the problem and what that understanding suggests for the action to take is even more important.

Part of understanding a problem involves the context in which you view the situation. The context that will work best for nearly all team problems is the *systems view*. This view suggests looking at interactions and interdependencies and how those affect what happens to bring about a problem.

The team problem solving process described here has seven steps. By taking time on the first three steps in the process, the team improves the chances the last four will yield a solution and results that the team is looking for. Figure 14.1 shows the steps in this process.

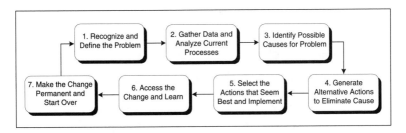

Figure 14.1   The steps in the problem solving process.

Generally the team will undertake the problem solving process as part of the team meetings. Each stage of the process will involve discussion and coming to various consensus decisions among team members. Individual members will also take on various assignments, usually involving gathering and analyzing information on some part of the problem, that they report back to the entire team.

Step 1: Recognize and Define the Problem

When the team encounters a problem, it will always have to do either with how its processes are operating or with some type of customer dissatisfaction. Processes should operate to minimize waste and costs, while delivering defect-free outputs that meet customer needs and expectations. When things get in the way of that happening, the team has a problem. So the primary part of defining the problem has to do with understanding what about the process is causing a problem or what about the output is not satisfying the customer.

Here are some problems that a team might encounter that will require some solution if the team doesn't want to see its performance compromised.

- Some percentage of the outputs from a process are regularly defective.

- The process bogs down at various points and the team is unable to meet its delivery dates.

- Accidents on the job have been occurring.

- Customer complaints about quality have increased.

- There have been communication breakdowns between teams working on interdependent processes.

- Suppliers have been late with deliveries or the parts supplied don't meet specifications.

STEP 2: COLLECT INFORMATION AND ANALYZE CURRENT PROCESSES

Now that the team has defined the nature of the problem, they need to gather information that will help them better understand what's going on. For example, if customers are complaining, the team might collect information about what specifically is wrong—defective products, untimely delivery, and so on.

The team will also need to look at how the current processes are operating. By understanding these processes that are involved in the problem, the team begins to think about what changes would be appropriate to effectively address the problem. Such analysis would likely involve the development of a flowchart showing current process steps. It can also involve determining who is responsible for these, the sequence of operations, and the interdependencies among different steps and tasks.

This step could also involve the use of other process management tools, such as histograms, Pareto charts, and control charts, all with the goal of better understanding how the current process operates.

Step 3: Identify Possible Causes for the Problem

Problem solving means just that—solving the problem so it doesn't recur. This means getting at its root cause rather than just dealing with some symptom. Many times, the reason for a problem is not initially obvious. Or it could be the result of a variety of causes that come together in a way that compromises team performance.

Cause-and-effect diagrams are a very good tool for exploring what might be happening in the system and its processes to cause a problem. The team might also use the five why techniques or it might use a scatter diagram to see correlations between factors that might bring about a problem.

Teams should resist the temptation to zero in on what might seem the obvious cause of a problem, such as a machine breaking down—fix the machine and no more problem. However, there are usually deeper reasons why such events happen that are only clear after exploring processes and what influences them.

STEP 4: GENERATE ALTERNATIVE ACTIONS TO ELIMINATE CAUSES

After the team has a clear sense of what the cause of the problem might be, then members can proceed to generate suggestions for how to address the cause and make changes that will solve the problem. Sometimes the changes will be obvious. For example, it may be that some members need training on a particular skill, such as using measurement devices, or that a machine's calibration is out of whack. Provide the training or fix the calibration, and process operations and outputs begin to meet expectations.

That's not always the case, however. It may require that the team brainstorm to come up with various ideas that will permanently solve the problem. In thinking about the problem and its causes, here are some questions the team can use to generate suggested actions:

- **Are these processes in statistical control?** This question helps the team determine whether a problem has a special cause that can be addressed immediately or is the result of common causes within the system that will require more detailed examination.

- **Does our proposed solution address symptoms or does it get to the root cause of the problem?** This question keeps the team away from the temptation of temporarily solving the problem rather than taking actions that will prevent it from ever happening again.

- **Are we basing our suggestions on factual data or opinions?** This question keeps the team using facts about the process rather than speculating about the nature of the problem and its potential solutions.

- **Will the proposed change keep customers satisfied as well as improve internal operations?** This question keeps the team focused both on the internal situation and on making sure customer satisfaction is maintained.

Step 5: Select the Actions that Seem Best and Implement Them

At this point in the process, the team should have a good sense of the feasibility of each alternative in terms of its effect on the team and its processes and the achievement of organizational goals. All the steps before this represent the "understanding the problem" part of the process. Once the team has carefully gone through the understanding steps, the best alternative will often become apparent, and that's the one the team selects.

If there is general agreement that the course of action selected will solve the problem the team needs to come up with a plan for implementing it. This plan will include *who* will do *what* by *when* and what *resources* and *funds* are needed. The team then proceeds to execute the plan, which leads to the next step.

It may be, however, that the team is not clear about whether the solution they have agreed on will work. In that case, they may want to pilot their solution in one part of the process and monitor the results to see if they get the results they expect. They can learn from the pilot, make any appropriate changes, and roll it out for the entire set of processes.

A **pilot** is a small-scale trial of a new process or procedure to see if it works before implementing it on a final basis.

An example of a pilot solution might involve changes to a product that make it easier to manufacture but the team wants to be sure it still meets customer needs. They develop a trial of the change and check customer reactions. If that works, then the change becomes permanent.

STEP 6: ASSESS THE CHANGE AND LEARN

We've already previewed this step in our discussion of piloting a change. A team will inevitably find that any set of actions they implement will not work out just as they expected. The team cannot anticipate all the results of implementing a change, so they need to collect data, using tools such as control charts, that show how well the process with changes is operating.

They need to ask questions such as:

- Are defects as a percent of outputs down?
- Does the process now deliver outputs on time?
- Have costs been reduced?
- Are customers more satisfied?

The team members need to collect factual data that lets them know how well their solution is working. They need to capture what they have learned from this experience. They can use this learning to make sure the problem doesn't happen again and make further refinements to the solution they selected.

STEP 7: MAKE THE CHANGE PERMANENT AND START OVER

The last step is the "standardizing" of the change, making it a permanent part of operations. This includes communication and documentation of the new procedure as well as any training that might be appropriate.

Along with making it permanent, it also involves the continuing collection of data to measure how the revised process is operating and continuing to look for problems and opportunities to improve.

The team should continue to use the process management tools described in lessons 12 and 13. Only by staying on top of processes can the team assure that the change stays permanent as well as catch other problems as they occur.

In this lesson, you learned a 7-step method that teams can use to understand and solve process problems. In the next lesson, you will learn about problems that undermine team success and what to do about them.

WHY TEAMS
DON'T WORK
AND WHAT TO DO
ABOUT IT

In this lesson, you will learn about why organizations have problems implementing teams, what some of these problems are, and how to deal with them and take actions that assure team success.

There is a reason why nearly every company in the Fortune 500 and lots more have instituted teams. Teams are more effective at executing and improving processes, reducing costs, and building a committed workforce. That sounds great, doesn't it? However, it's not that easy. There are lots of opportunities for team initiatives in organizations to go south. The result is frustrated managers, frustrated employees, and no real difference in performance from the old hierarchy, boss-subordinate days.

There are two fundamental reasons why teams don't work in organizations:

- Management problems
- Team member problems

In considering these, it's useful to remember that both problems feed off the other. Let's examine both of these.

MANAGEMENT-CAUSED TEAM PROBLEMS

Management isn't always to blame for why teams fail to produce expected results, but it certainly plays an important role. Here are some ways management influences team performance, for better or for worse:

- **Management creates the culture in which teams will either prosper or falter.** If the culture does not support open communication, cooperation, and delegation of authority and responsibility to the people doing the work, teamwork is not going to happen.

> The culture is the employees' environment. Management creates and perpetuates the environment. If the environment is not one in which there is a premium on teamwork values (see Lesson 2), then high-performing teams will never take root.

- **Management institutes teams but doesn't provide for teamwork training.** Just because a company calls a group of people who work together a team doesn't mean they are a team. Training in interpersonal communication, decision making, meeting skills, and the tools of process management are all required if teams are to succeed. If management is not ready to commit to such training, teams will falter.

- **Management does not change the compensation system.** Most approaches to compensation in traditional, non-team oriented organizations focus on individual performance and even reward employees who look good in relation to their peers. If employees see that there is no compensation for performing as a team (rather than as individuals), then they aren't going to take teamwork seriously.

- **Management does not clearly articulate team boundaries and goals.** For a team to perform well, it has to have a clear sense of its purpose and responsibilities. With those in place and with the confidence that management is there to support the team in accomplishing its goals, it will thrive. With only a vague sense of purpose and little support, it will have serious problems.

- **Management institutes teams for activities in which teams are not necessarily appropriate.** Teams are not always necessary for all organizational activities. For example, a team may not be appropriate in a customer service operation, where each person responds to customer questions. Team activities can take time away from answering phones, but don't make people more efficient. In this case, team members quickly become disenchanted with being on the team.

- **Management must provide on-going leadership and support of the team initiative.** Employees must believe that management is there to help them succeed and will provide the resources and information the team needs to accomplish its mission. Without on-going leadership and support from management, members of the team will not take participation seriously.

> When a company is getting teams underway, management has to expect it will take some time for the team to start performing at a high level. Without patience and a long-term commitment to teams, the handwriting is on the wall for failure.

If it's not clear already, the way to correct management-caused team problems is commitment to training and developing a culture, compensation program, and support system that will serve as a solid foundation for teamwork. Management also must be willing to take the long view that teams will work. After all, a movement to teams is not a quick fix. It's simply the intelligent thing to do to better manage processes and satisfy customers.

It's important to appreciate, however, that the intelligence of this lies in taking the systems view of organizations. This view naturally motivates the attitudes and actions that will support teams and teamwork and help assure that problems such as those mentioned previously will not occur. On the other hand, without this view, you can be sure that the company will have the types of team problems described here and more.

TEAM-CAUSED TEAM PROBLEMS

It's clear that management mistakes and the lack of a supporting teamwork culture are often at the heart of the failure of teams to live up to expectations. Sometimes, however, the team members themselves also make mistakes that undermine performance. Let's review some of the mistakes teams make. (The ideas in this section were adapted from, among other sources, the article "When Is a Team Its Own Worst Enemy?", *Training*, Sept. 1995, pp. 71–82.)

Unrealistic Expectations

Sometimes when a team is instituted, with the all the accompanying hoopla, the team members will have an unrealistic understanding of what its responsibilities and capabilities are. Team members may want to interact with customers and suppliers and take on other responsibilities that aren't in the cards. The result is a letdown and disappointment and a lack of commitment that undermines the team's chances of succeeding.

The most effective way to deal with this problem is to make sure the team knows its responsibilities and the boundaries of its authority. Team members should also have a clear sense of the team concept from the systems perspective and what it means in terms of better executing and improving their processes. But don't make the move to teams seem like a panacea. Team members will continue to work on their particular tasks, but with the added skills that come from training in teamwork and process management.

Too Much Too Soon

This is related to unrealistic expectations. When a company begins a transition to teams with the ultimate goal of self-directed teams, early on, members may want to do more than they are actually capable of. They learn about advanced teams taking charge of a whole range of activities including hiring, purchasing, and other duties. They may want to take these on before they are ready and find they don't have the skills or insight to perform them well. This naturally leads to frustration and disappointment and the team can fall apart.

Refer to Lesson 9 and the path to self-direction. Teams need to move through several stages of sophistication before they take on the tasks that managers traditionally handle.

The best way to prevent this type of problem from happening is to make sure teams understand how self-direction evolves and provide the training in a sequence that will lead them along at the right pace. In this way, increasing team member skills and responsibilities will match up with one another.

DIFFERENT WORK STYLES INTERFERE WITH COOPERATION

Some team members may be fast learners and very skilled at their tasks. Others may be slower and less proficient on the job. Such differences can cause conflicts that interfere with the cooperation that is at the heart of why teams exist in the first place. For example, if one team member depends on another to complete a task by a certain time, and it regularly doesn't happen, teamwork suffers and members lose confidence in the idea of the team in the first place.

Some ways to avoid or deal with this type of problem include:

- Have performance standards in place that team members understand. The goal here is to make sure that all team members can perform in a way that facilitates cooperation.

- Give team members jobs that are appropriate to their skills and work styles.

- Create a team environment characterized by open communication. In this way, team members can talk to each other and work out such problems.

TOO OCCUPIED WITH WORK TO TALK

Sometimes teams become so obsessed with their goals and results that they push themselves very hard to achieve them. Team members may feel that meetings and any other unnecessary communication will get in the way of their performance. After some time, members start to blame each other when things don't go as expected (as they inevitably won't).

 If the team has an obsession with goals and results, it's probably because management has the same focus. Unless cooperation to achieve goals and the necessary communication that fosters cooperation are in place, teamwork will suffer. And when teamwork suffers, so, ultimately, does performance.

The way to handle this potential problem is to place an emphasis on having at least one weekly team meeting as well as open communication and cooperative problem solving. Meetings let everyone know what's going on, what they need to do, and how their work affects that of other team members. The cooperation, communication, and intelligent application of process management tools facilitated by meetings will, in the final analysis, make it easier for teams to reach their goals with fewer problems.

NONPERFORMERS ON THE TEAM

Sometimes no matter how much the team and the company does to support teamwork, some members just don't get it, at least initially. Some people won't be able to do the work and won't feel comfortable in a team setting. This can undermine the morale of other members and get them focusing more on the nonperforming members than on working together to achieve goals.

Starting with the assumption that it's better to help than to fire, some ways to deal with nonperformers include:

- Have the team leader spend more time working with the nonperforming individual to help this individual gain the skills and performance feedback needed to improve.

- Have a job rotation program where team members learn all the jobs as well as a better appreciation of the interdependence of jobs. This can help the nonperformer see the light and improve.

- Provide special training that this individual may need to come up to speed.

Sometimes such efforts just don't yield results, and the nonperformer will need to be reassigned or perhaps, as a last resort, terminated. For the sake of the team and the company, it may be better to terminate the individual—but only after the team leader and other members take actions to bring him or her around.

THE KEYS TO DEALING WITH TEAMWORK PROBLEMS

The most important thing management and teams can do to solve problems is to take actions that prevent many of them from occurring the first place. If you review the different types of problems covered in this lesson, you will find that many of them come from management and from team members not properly understanding what instituting teams and being on a team really involves.

As noted throughout this book, the teamwork culture and attitude are vital to success. So is training. With an understanding of why teams make sense and how they evolve and an open-eyed view of what's required to participate as a team member, it's far more likely they will succeed.

However, neither managers nor team members can anticipate all the problems that might get in the way of a team succeeding. When problems arise, such as interpersonal or other types of conflicts or any of hundreds of everyday process problems, the teams that succeed face these head on, collect data, and use an agreed-on problem-solving approach to solve them. It's really not the problems that undermine team performance, but either the inability or lack of desire to deal with them.

One hallmark of every successful team is the ability to confront and quickly solve problems when they occur. Another is for the team to understand processes well enough to prevent problems, especially those that relate to how the team members work together, from ever happening in the first place.

Finally, there is only one reason to implement teams in any organization: they help people, whose work is already interdependent, work together better. If managers, team leaders, and team members understand this, deeply understand it, then the types of problems reviewed here are less likely to happen. And if they do occur, everyone will be able to deal with them better, learn from the experience, and continuously improve their performance.

In this lesson, you learned about why organizations have problems implementing teams, what some of these problems are, and how to take actions to deal with them and assure team success.

INDEX

U - V

W - Z